DISTINCTLY KENTUCKY

A Coloring Book

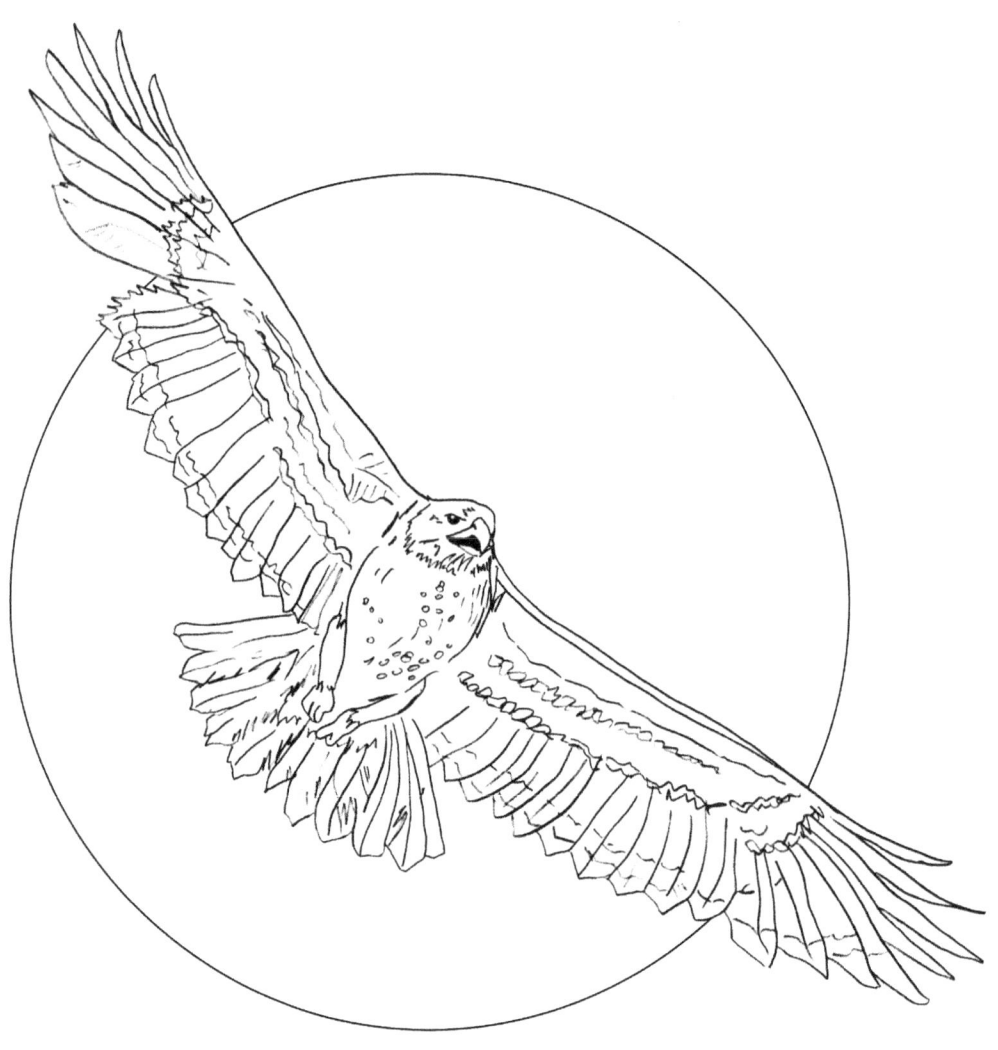

DISTINCTLY KENTUCKY

COLORING BOOK

Drawings
by Robert A. Powell

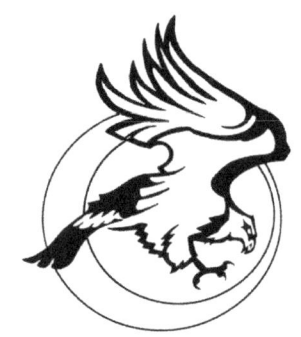

Published & Distributed by:

Silverhawke Publications

ISBN 9781090751089

Copyright 2019 by Robert A. Powell

CONTENTS

Distinctly Kentucky!

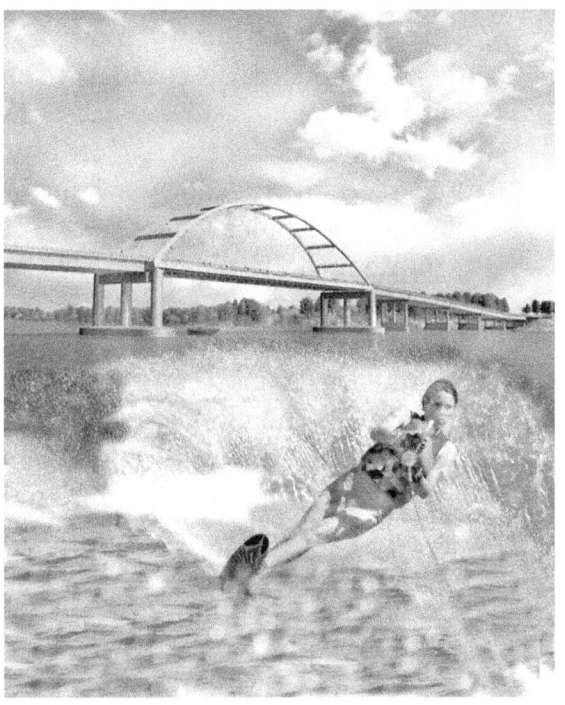

To best represent the exciting colorful heritage of our great state, I selected subjects from each of the geographic regions of Kentucky as well as a balance of landmarks, activities, symbols, and natural wonders from every designated region in the Kentucky Tourism guide. Although many of the subjects may be similar to ones found in other parts of the country, every unique picture in this book is *distinctly Kentucky*.

Kentucky (kən-TUK-ee) is a state located in the east south-central region of the United States. According to the law creating it, Kentucky is officially the *Commonwealth of Kentucky*, one of four states constituted as a commonwealth (the others are Virginia, Pennsylvania, and Massachusetts). It was originally a part of Virginia, but separated in 1792 to become the 15th state to join the Union. Today, half of the states include more people with Kentucky ranking 26th in population among the 50 states.

Kentucky is known as the "Bluegrass State," a nickname based on the bluegrass found in many of its pastures due to the fertile soil and limestone water. Kentucky is best known world-wide for horse racing, bourbon distilleries, moonshine, coal, bluegrass music, basketball, and Kentucky Fried Chicken.

The limestone water has long been cited as the primary reason that Kentucky is the perfect place to make bourbon, raise racehorses, and grow tobacco and corn.

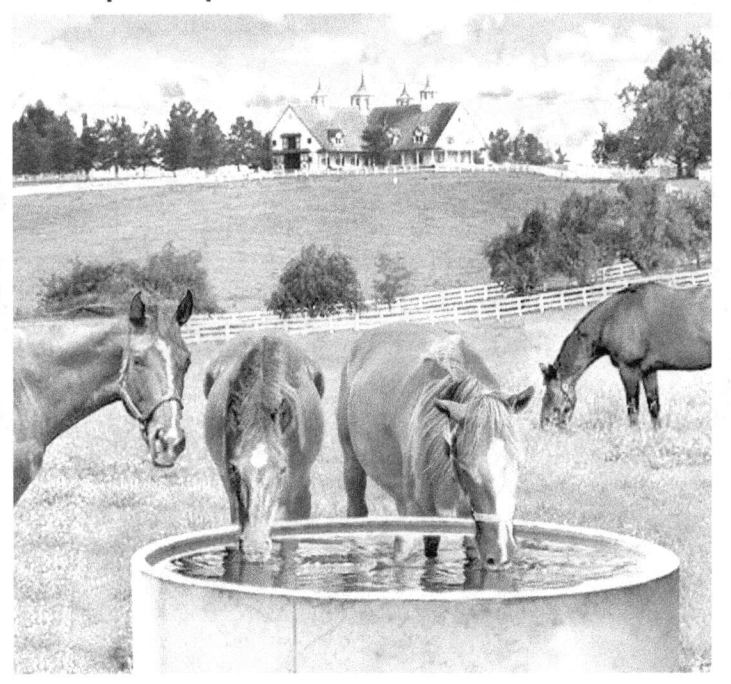

Limestone water is technically hard water with a high mineral content, formed when water percolates through deposits of limestone, which are largely made up of calcium and magnesium carbonates. However, no one has come up with a better explanation. Limestone filtered spring water is even bottled so that the gracious southern host or bourbon connoisseur might have "bourbon and branch" available. Master distillers claim that one splash of pure limestone water with your Kentucky bourbon will make an unbelievable difference. It is said to release all of the flavor and aroma nuances that make bourbon so uniquely popular.

The land offers diverse environments and abundant resources, including the longest cave system in the world, Mammoth Cave National Park. Kentucky also supports the greatest length of navigable waterways and streams (90,000 miles) in the contiguous United States, and the two largest man-made lakes east of the Mississippi River. Alaska is the only state with more miles of waterways.

In 1776, the area of Virginia west of the Appalachian Mountains became known as **Kentucky County**. No Native Americans were living in the region when the pioneers first entered in the 1700s, but five different Indian nations used the lands for hunting and as a sacred burying ground. None of them had a written language, but to those first frontiersmen who came in contact, it sounded like all of the Indians referred to the area as "Kentucke or Kaintuck". Even though the name stuck, the precise etymology of the word is uncertain. Most historians think it is based on an Iroquoian term meaning "the meadow" or "the prairie." In fact, Daniel Boone often referred to the area as the "Great Meadows."

Kentucky is situated in the Upland South, and a significant portion of eastern Kentucky is part of Appalachia.

Kentucky borders seven states. West Virginia lies to the east, Virginia to the southeast, Tennessee to the south, Missouri to the west, Illinois and Indiana to the northwest, and Ohio to the north and northeast. Only Missouri and Tennessee, both of which border eight states, touch more other states than Kentucky.

The northern border for Kentucky is formed by the Ohio River and its western border by the Mississippi River. The official state borders are based on the courses of the rivers as they existed when Kentucky became a state in 1792. Some parts of the river have changed since that time, and today, northbound travelers on U.S. 41 from Henderson will still be in Kentucky for about two miles, after crossing the Ohio River. Ellis Park is a thoroughbred racetrack located in this small piece of Kentucky.

Kentucky Bend is located in the far west corner of the state. It is actually an exclave that is surrounded completely by Missouri and Tennessee. It is included within the boundary of Fulton County. Road access to this small part of Kentucky requires travel through the state of Tennessee.

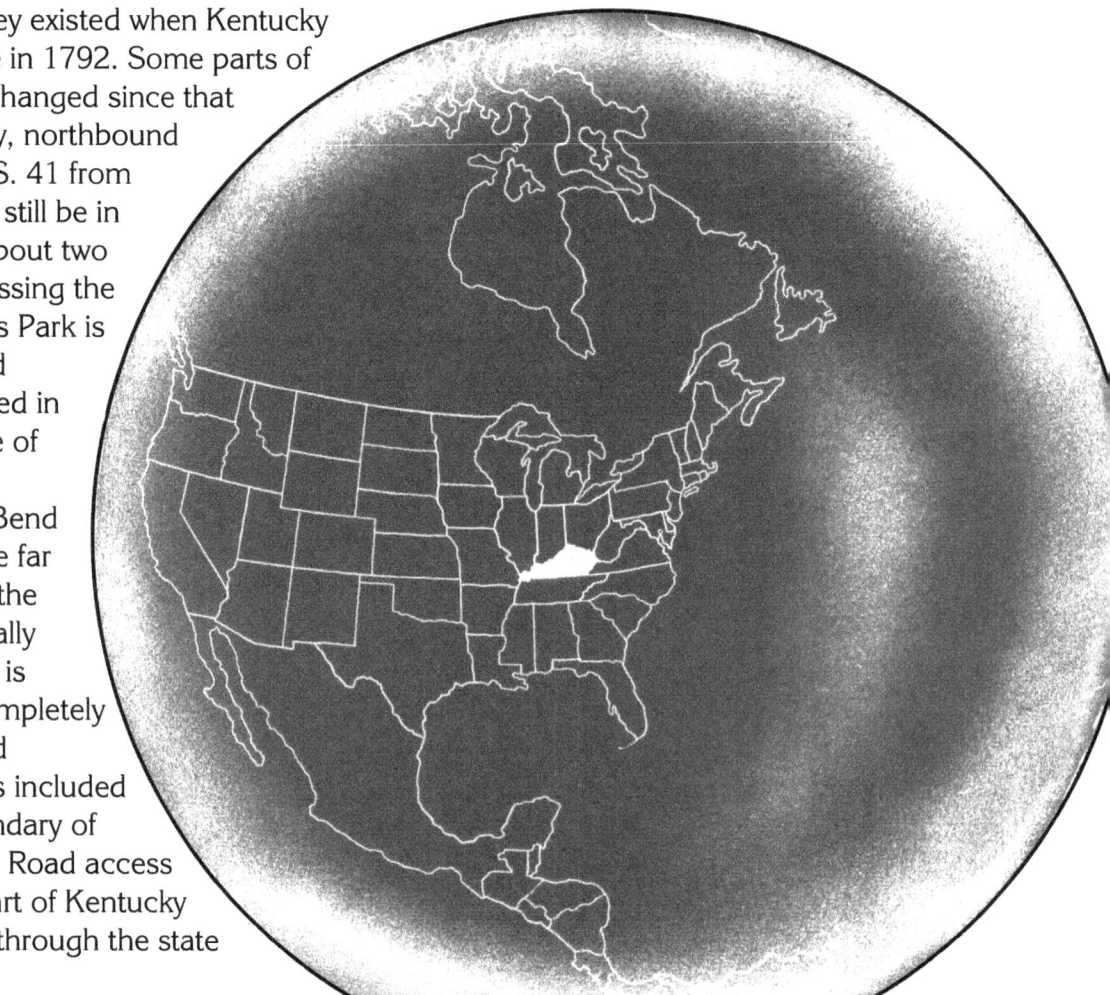

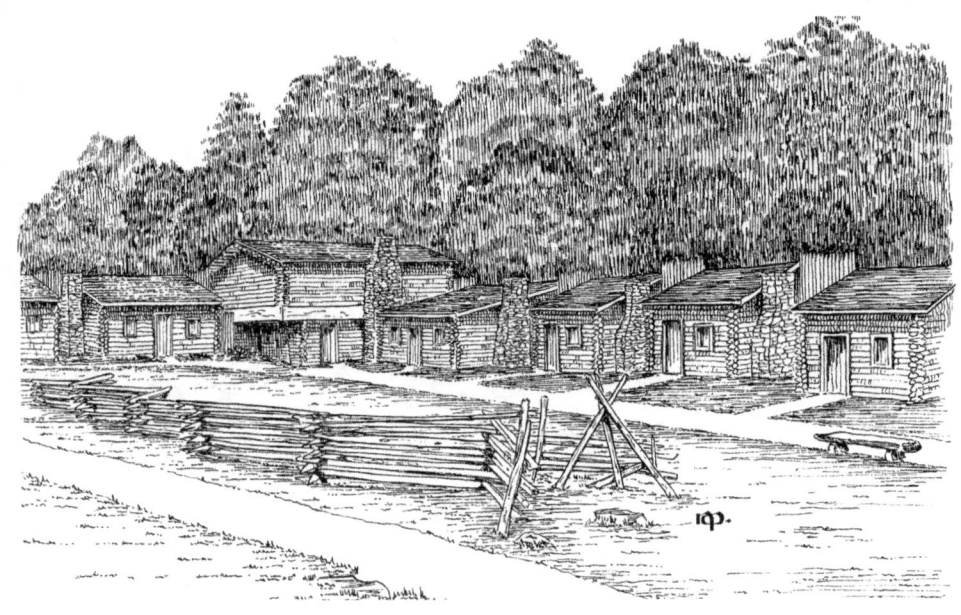

The epicenter of the powerful 1811-12 New Madrid earthquakes near this area, caused the Mississippi River to flow backwards in some places. The series of quakes did change the area geologically; however, the Kentucky Bend was formed because of a surveying error, not the earthquakes.

Kentucky is divided into five natural geographic regions: the Cumberland Plateau, the Bluegrass Region, the Pennyroyal Plateau (Pennyrile or Mississippi Plateau), the Western Coal Fields, and the Jackson Purchase. The Bluegrass Region consists of two major sections: the Inner Bluegrass encircles a 90-mile area around Lexington, and features hundreds of horse farms; the Outer Bluegrass contains most of the northern portion of the state, above the Knobs.

The Eastern Kentucky Coalfield is known for its extremely rugged terrain.

The Jackson Purchase and Pennyroyal are home to several bald cypress swamps.

Kentucky is the only U.S. state to have a continuous border of rivers running along three of its sides; the Mississippi River to the west, the Ohio River to the north, and the Big Sandy River and Tug Fork to the east. The major internal rivers include the Kentucky River, Tennessee River, Cumberland River, Green River and Licking River.

There are only three major natural lakes, but Kentucky is home to many man-made lakes. Kentucky has both the largest artificial lake east of the Mississippi in water volume (Lake Cumberland) and surface area (Kentucky Lake). Kentucky Lake has 2,064 miles of shoreline, 160,300 acres of water surface, and 4,008,000 acre feet of flood storage.

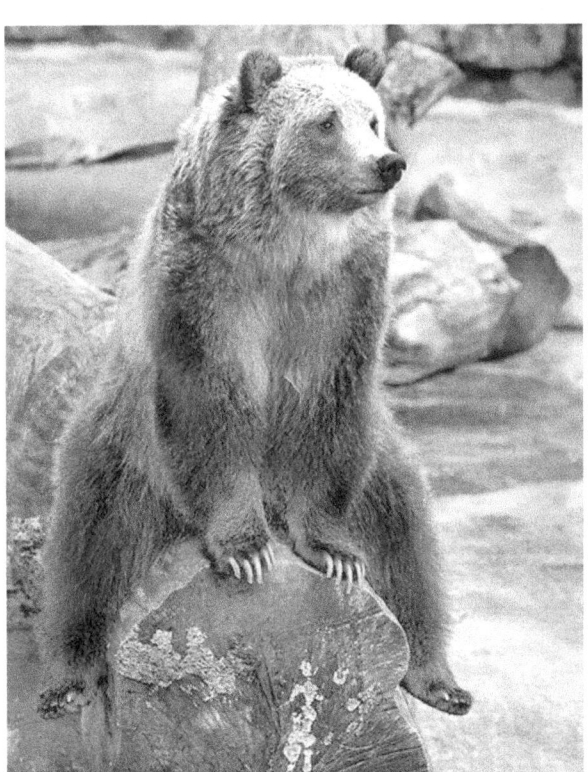

Kentucky has long been noted for its fantastic historic and natural parks. It boasts an expansive park system that includes one national park, two National Recreation areas, two National Historic Parks, two national forests, two National Wildlife Refuges, 45 state parks, 37,896 acres of state forest, and 82 Wildlife Management Areas.

The historic range of the American black bear was significantly reduced by habitat loss and fragmentation by the early 1900s. The return of black bears in Kentucky over the last 20 years is proving to be a true wildlife success story.

Kentucky has also been part of two of the most successful wildlife reintroduction projects in United States history. In 1997, the Kentucky Department of Fish and Wildlife Resources began to re-stock elk in the eastern counties, which had been extinct from the area for over 150 years. The state also stocked wild turkeys in the 1950s. There were reported to be less than 900 at one point. Once nearly extinct here, wild turkeys now thrive by the thousands across the state.

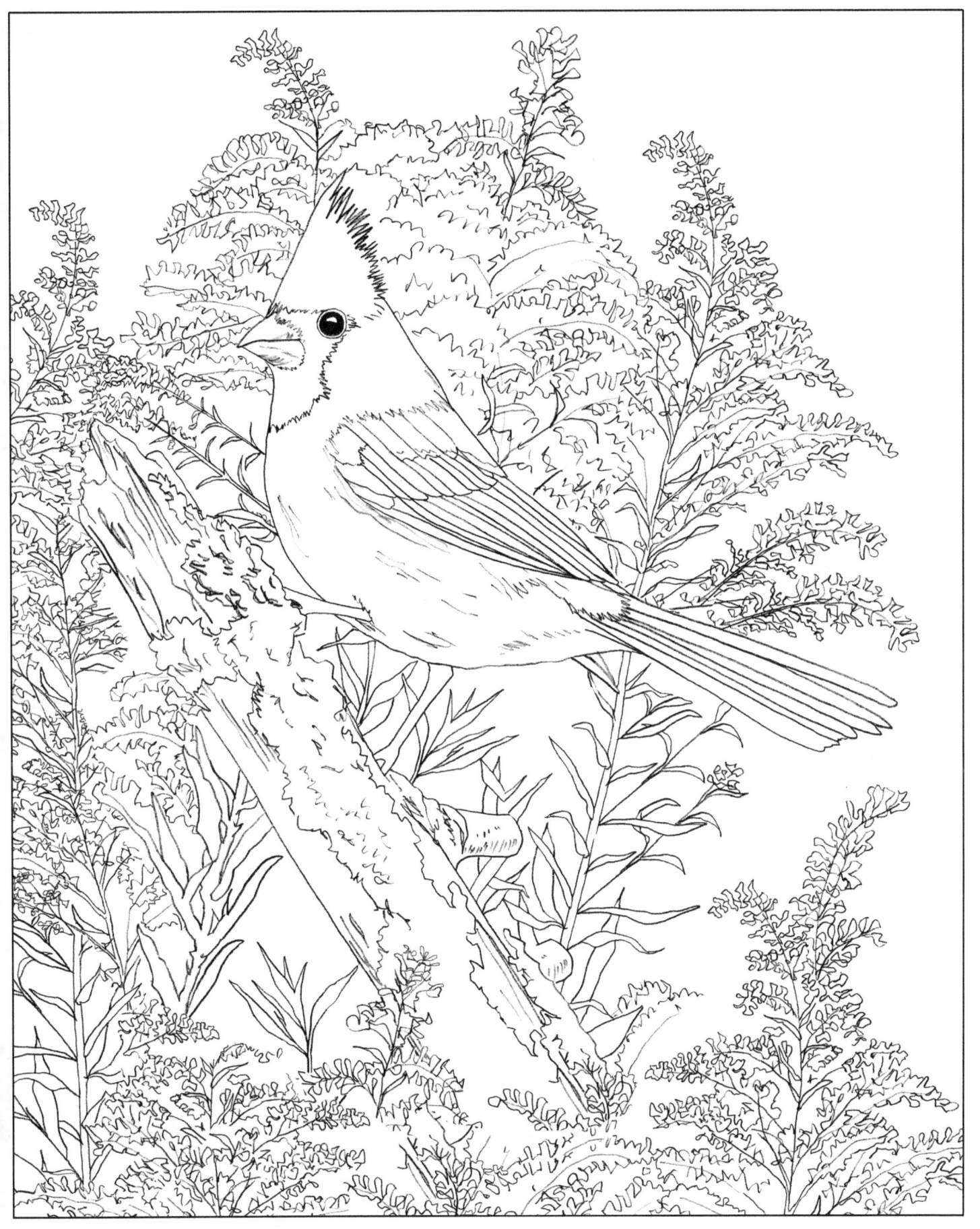

Cardinal on Goldenrod

State bird ★ State flower

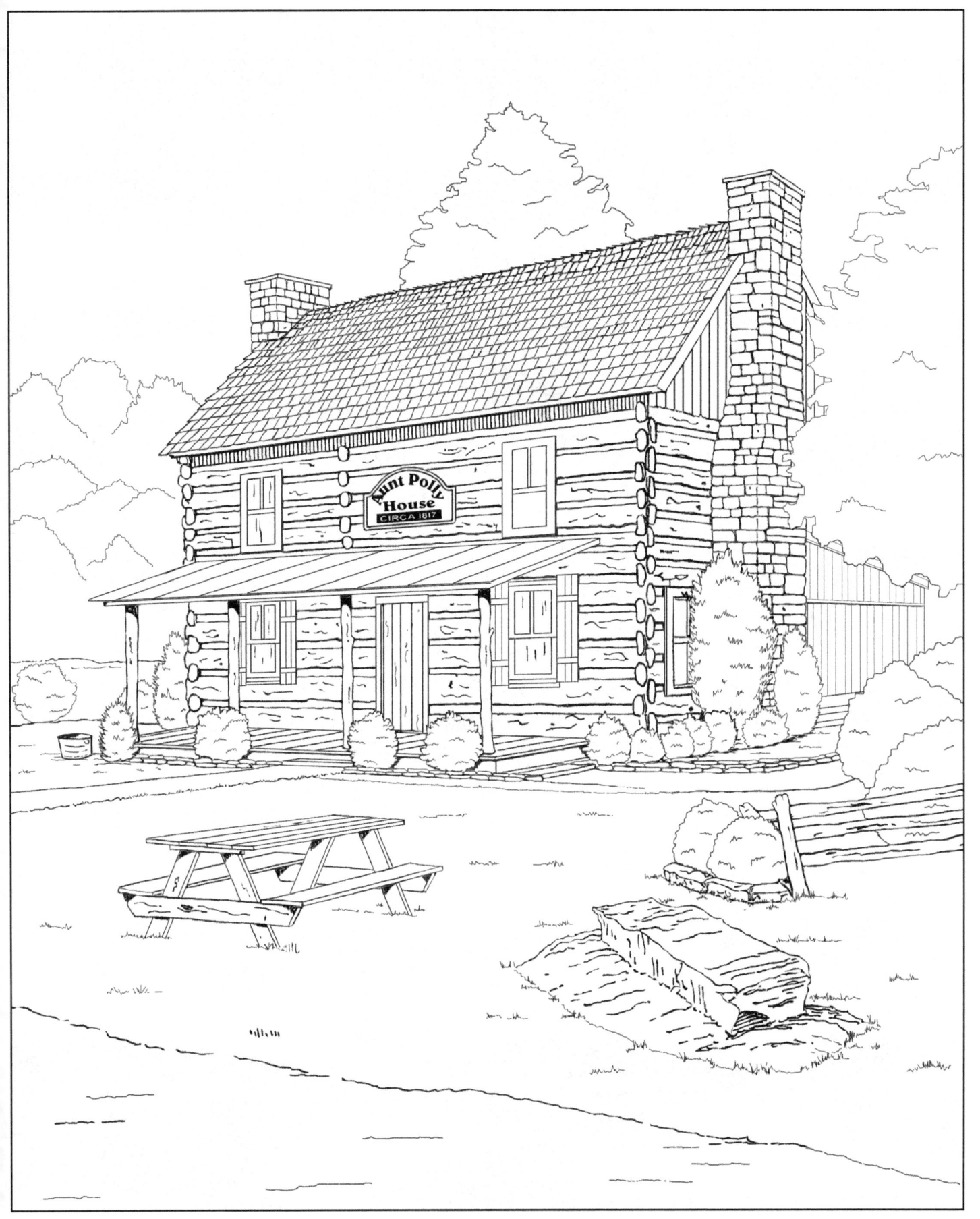

Aunt Polly House

Renfro Valley ★ Rockcastle County

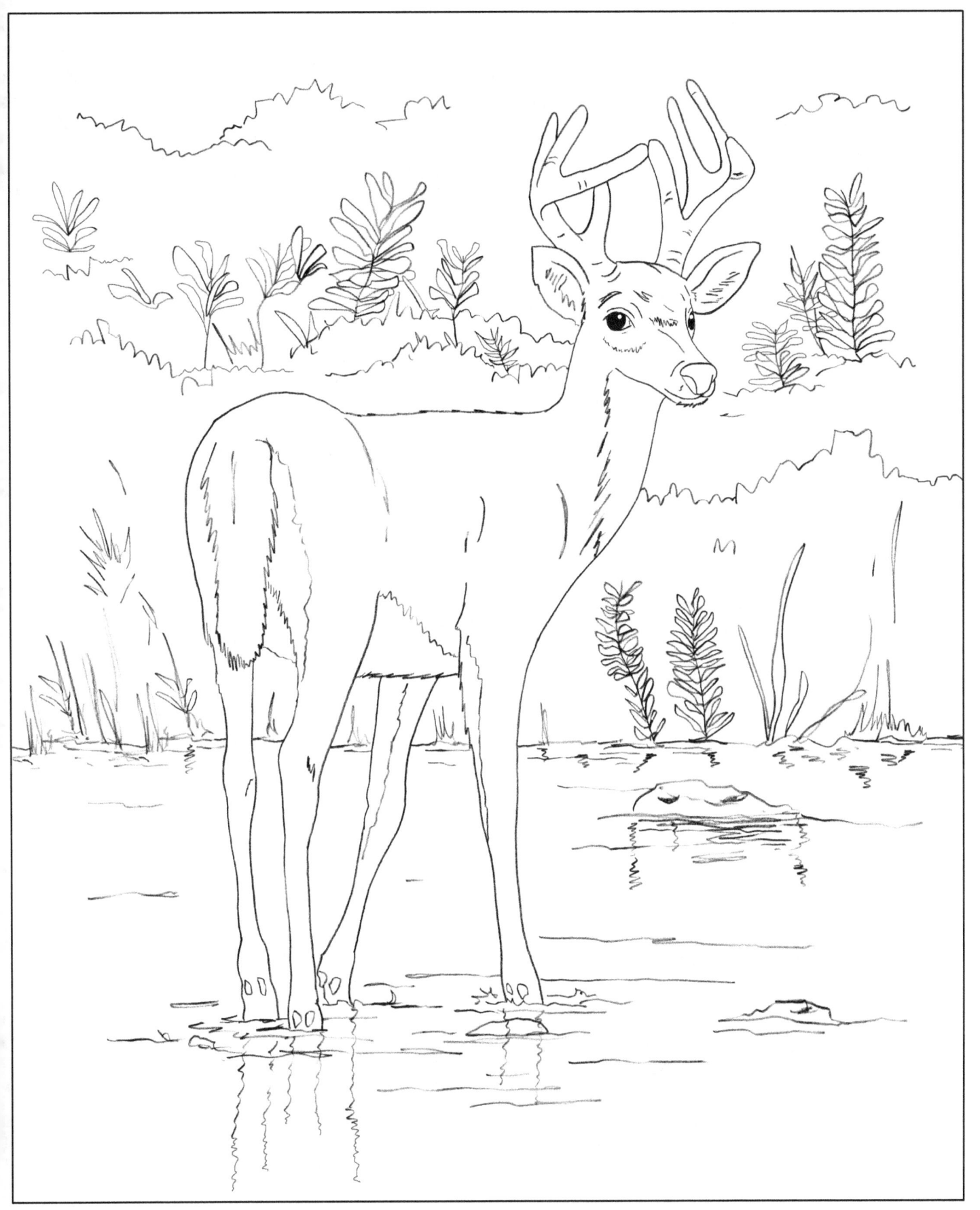

Kentucky Deer

Elk Creek Hunt Club ★ Owenton

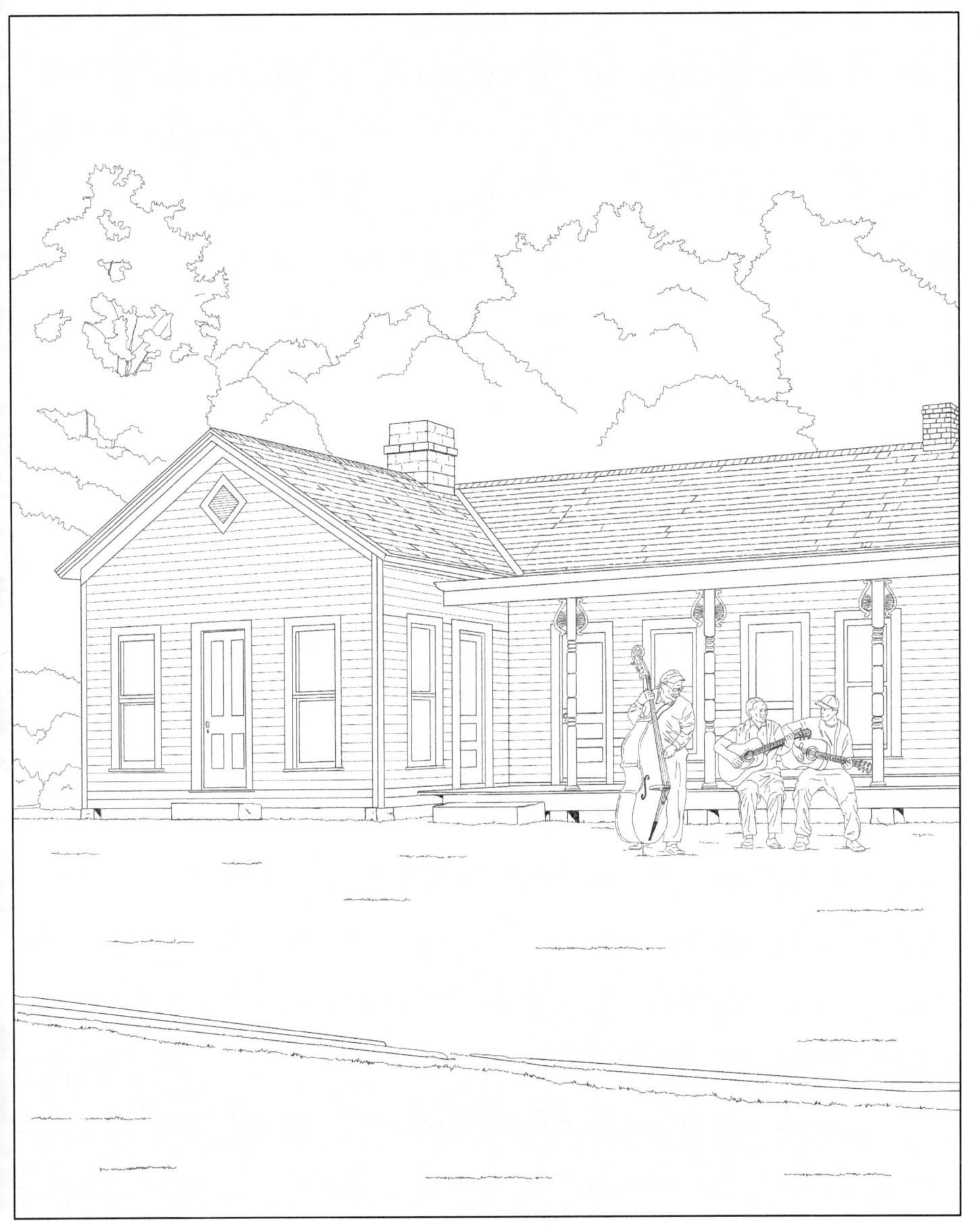

Monroe Homeplace

Pigeon Ridge ★ Ohio County

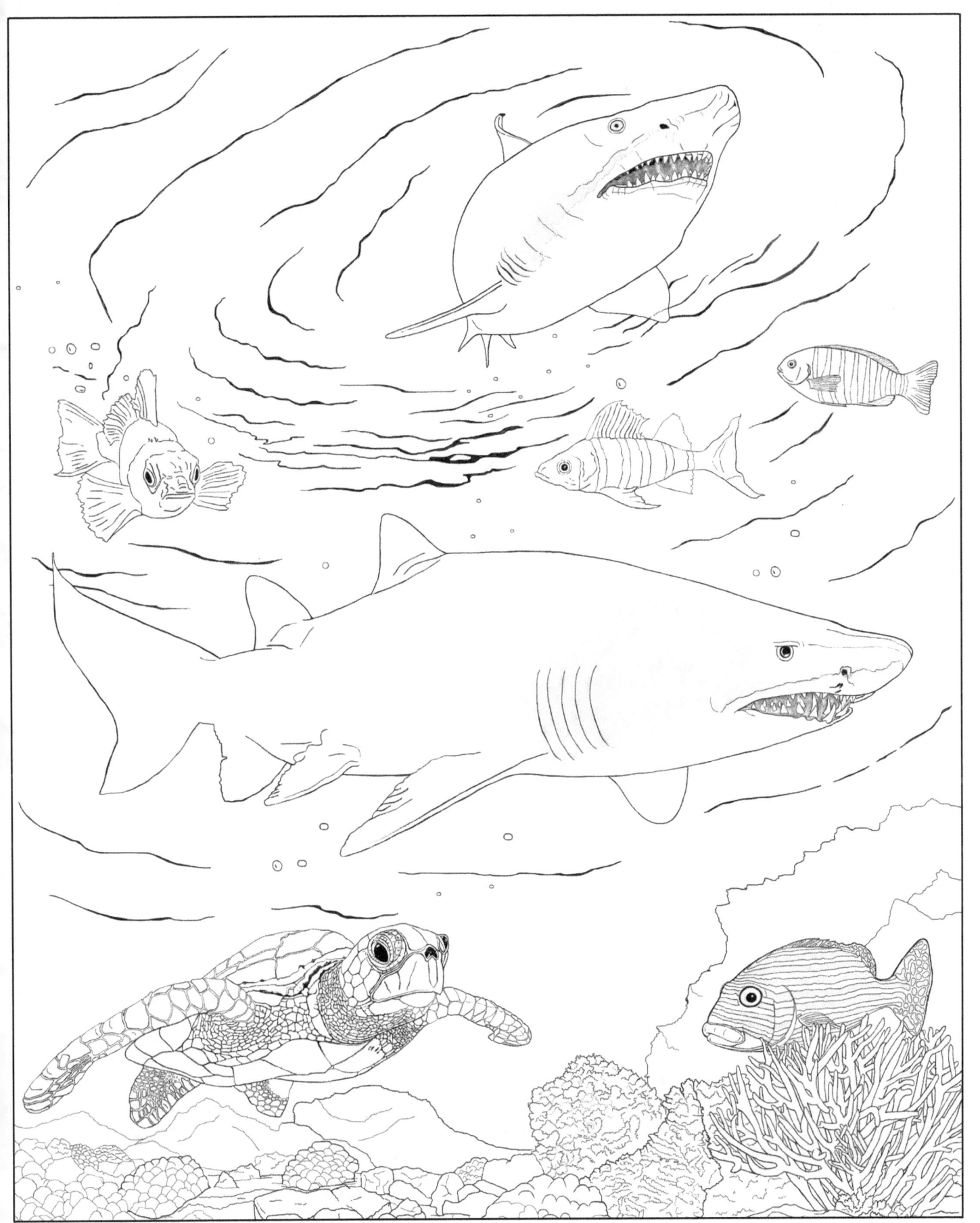

Newport Aquarium

Newport on the Levee ★ Campbell County

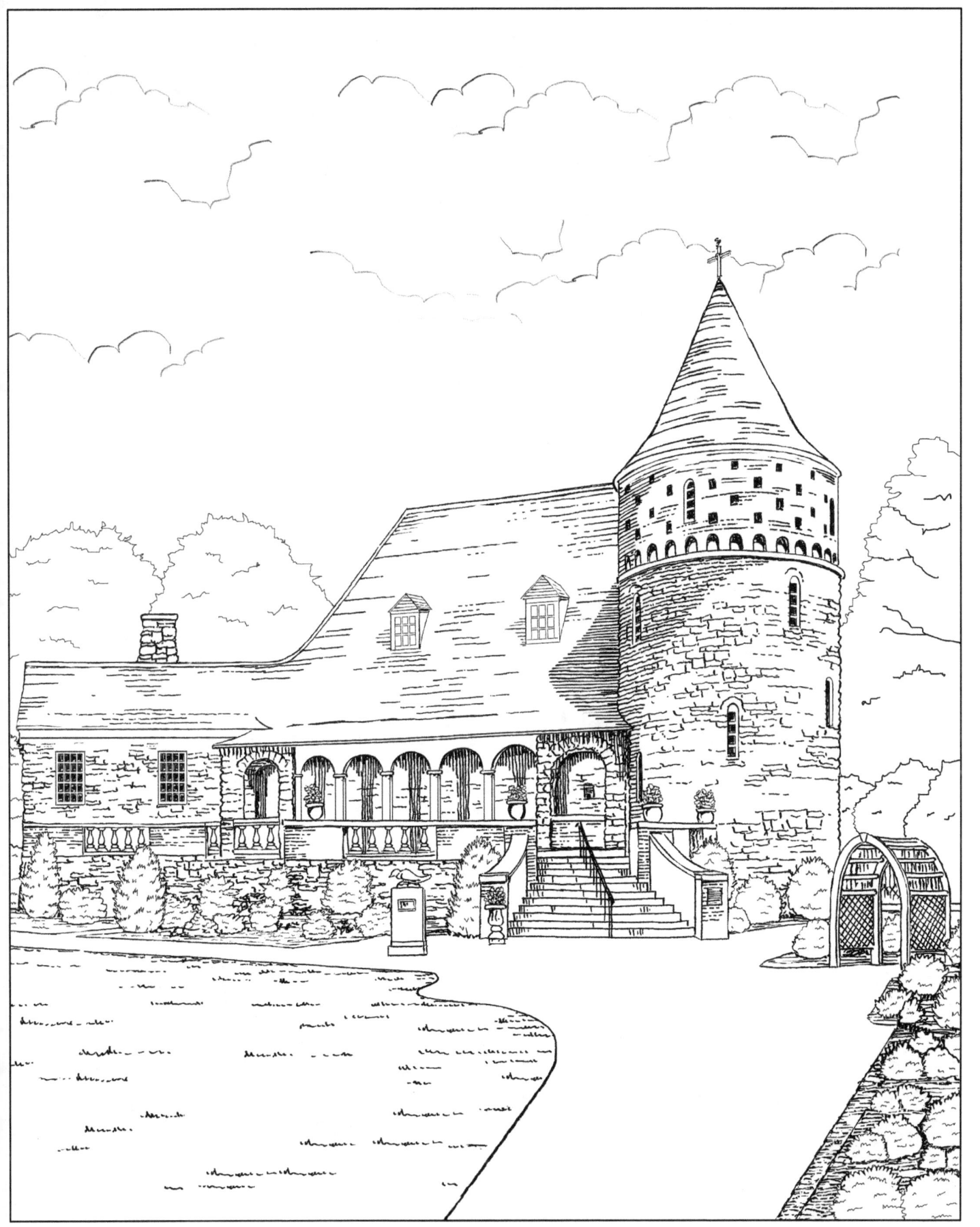

Audubon Museum

Henderson ★ Henderson County

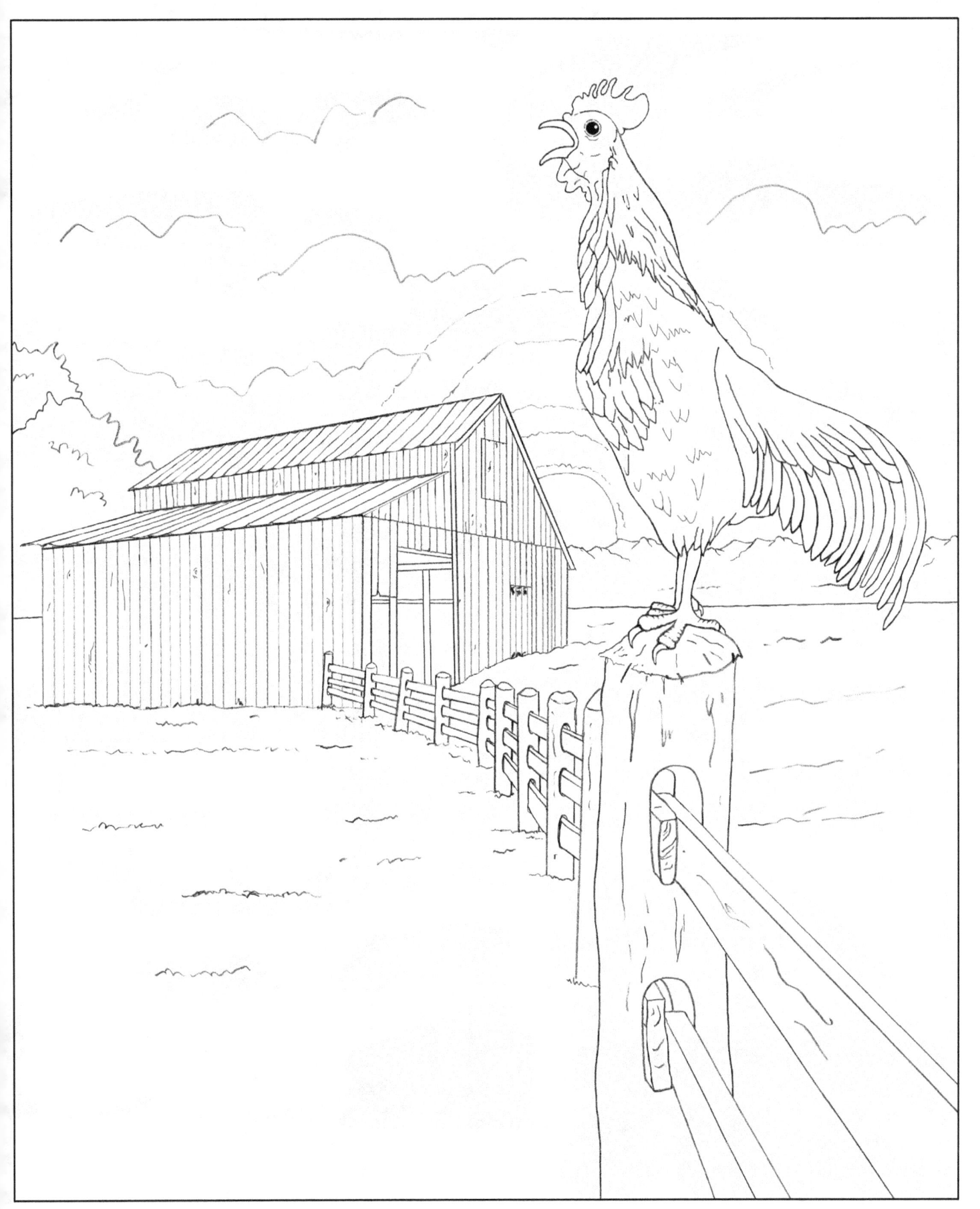

Kentucky Sunrise

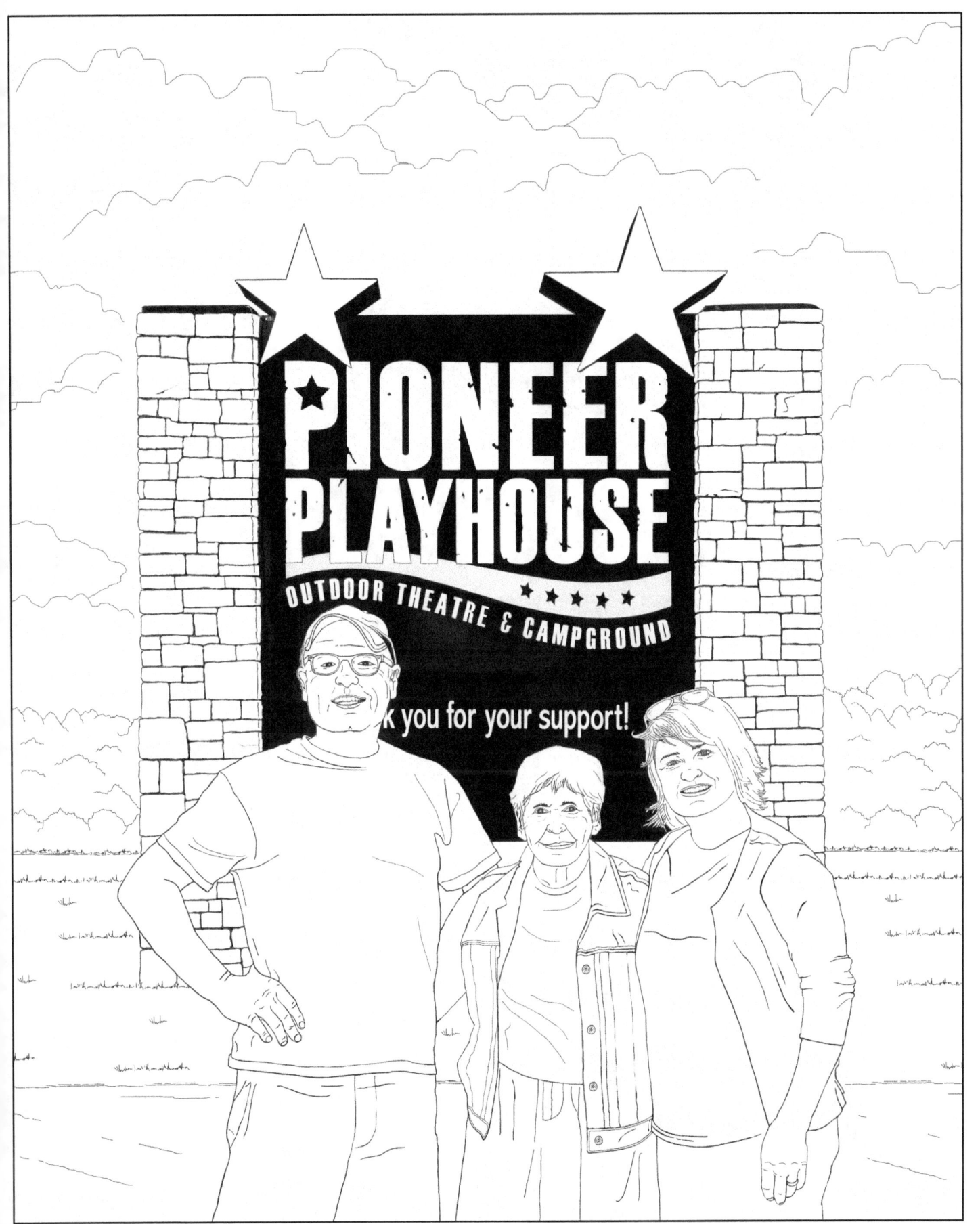

Pioneer Playhouse

Kentucky's Oldest Outdoor Theatre ★ Danville/ Boyle County

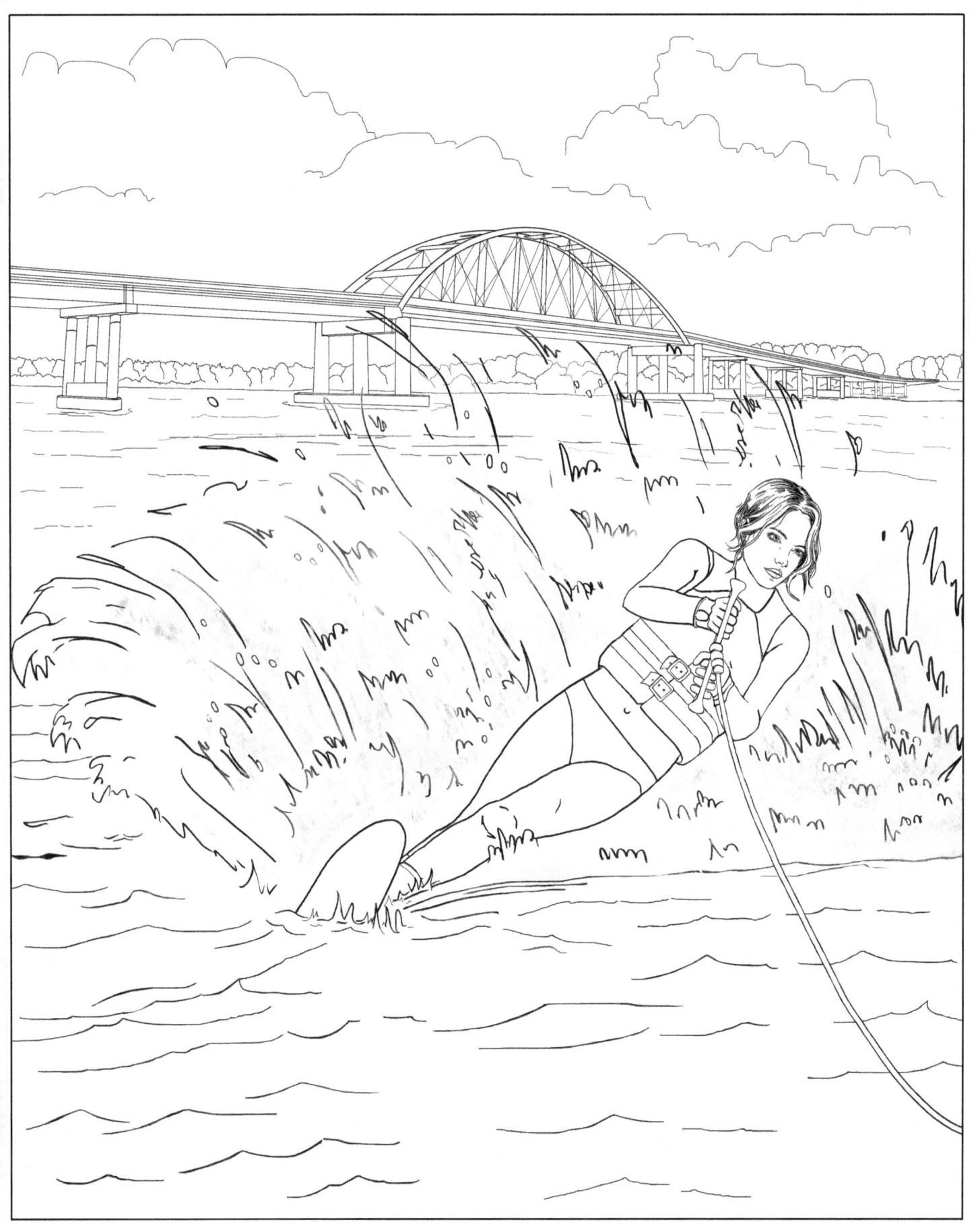

Kentucky Lake

Kentucky Lake Bridge at Aurora

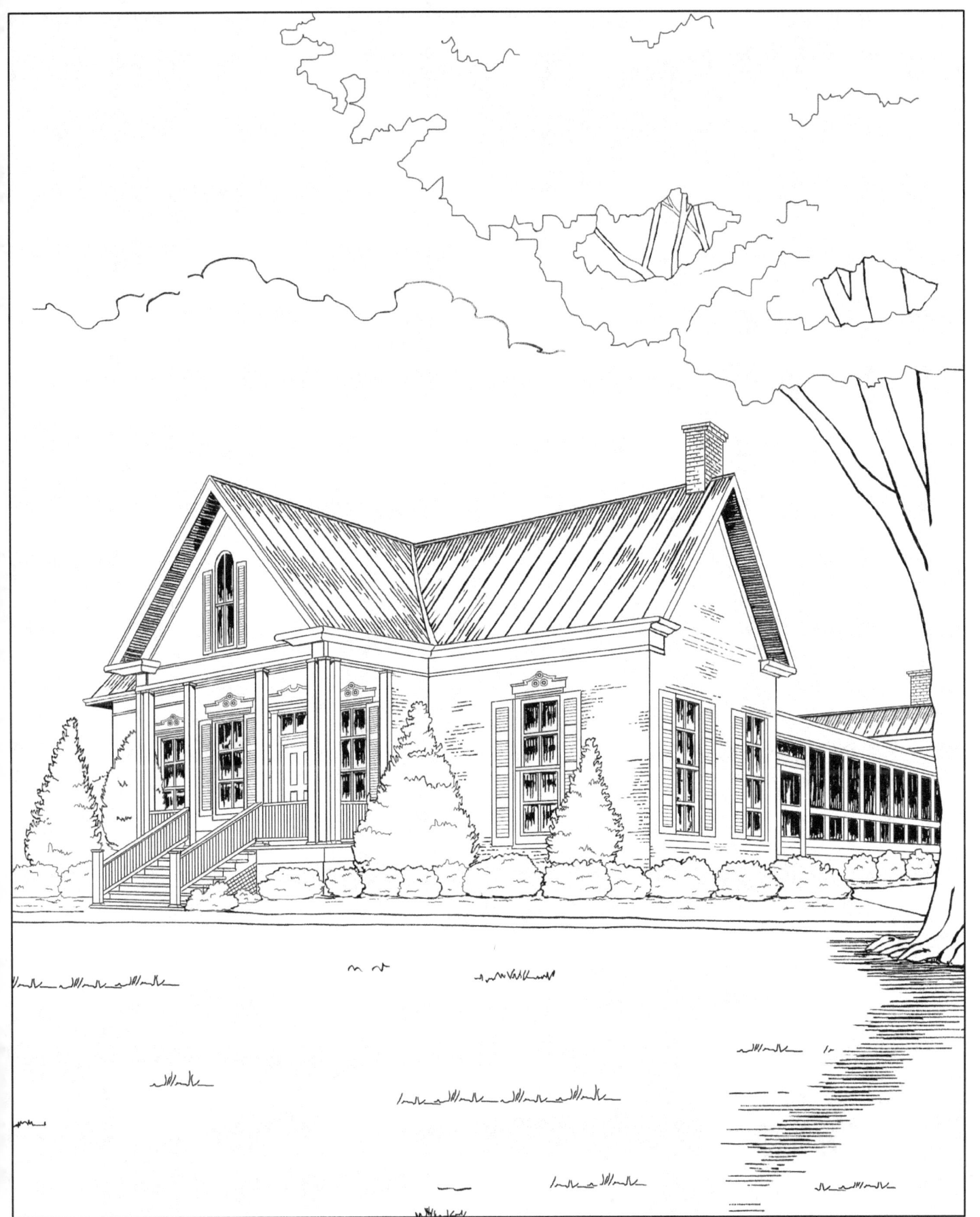

Angles

Home of Alben Barkley ★ Paducah/ McCracken County

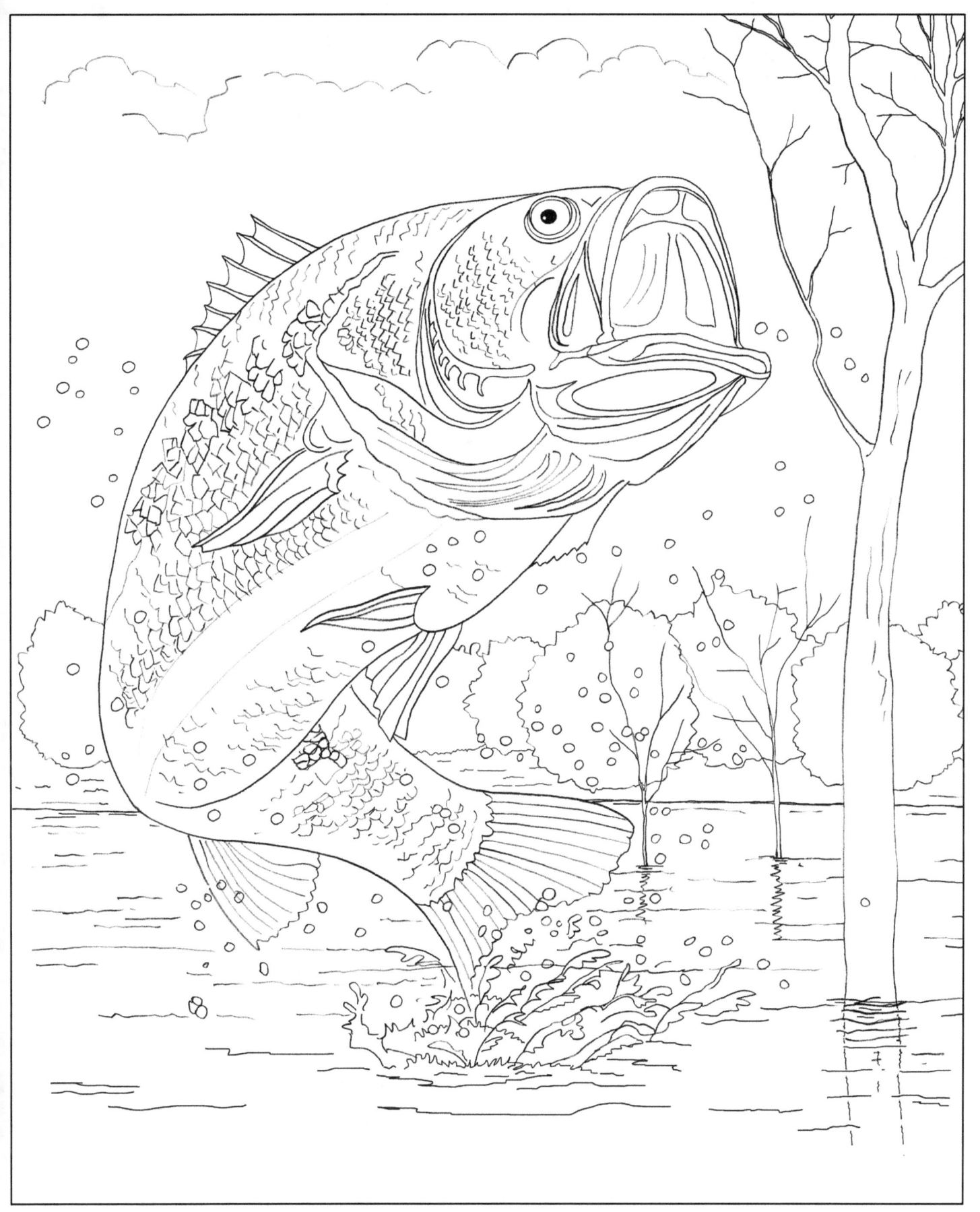

Kentucky Spotted Bass

State fish of Kentucky

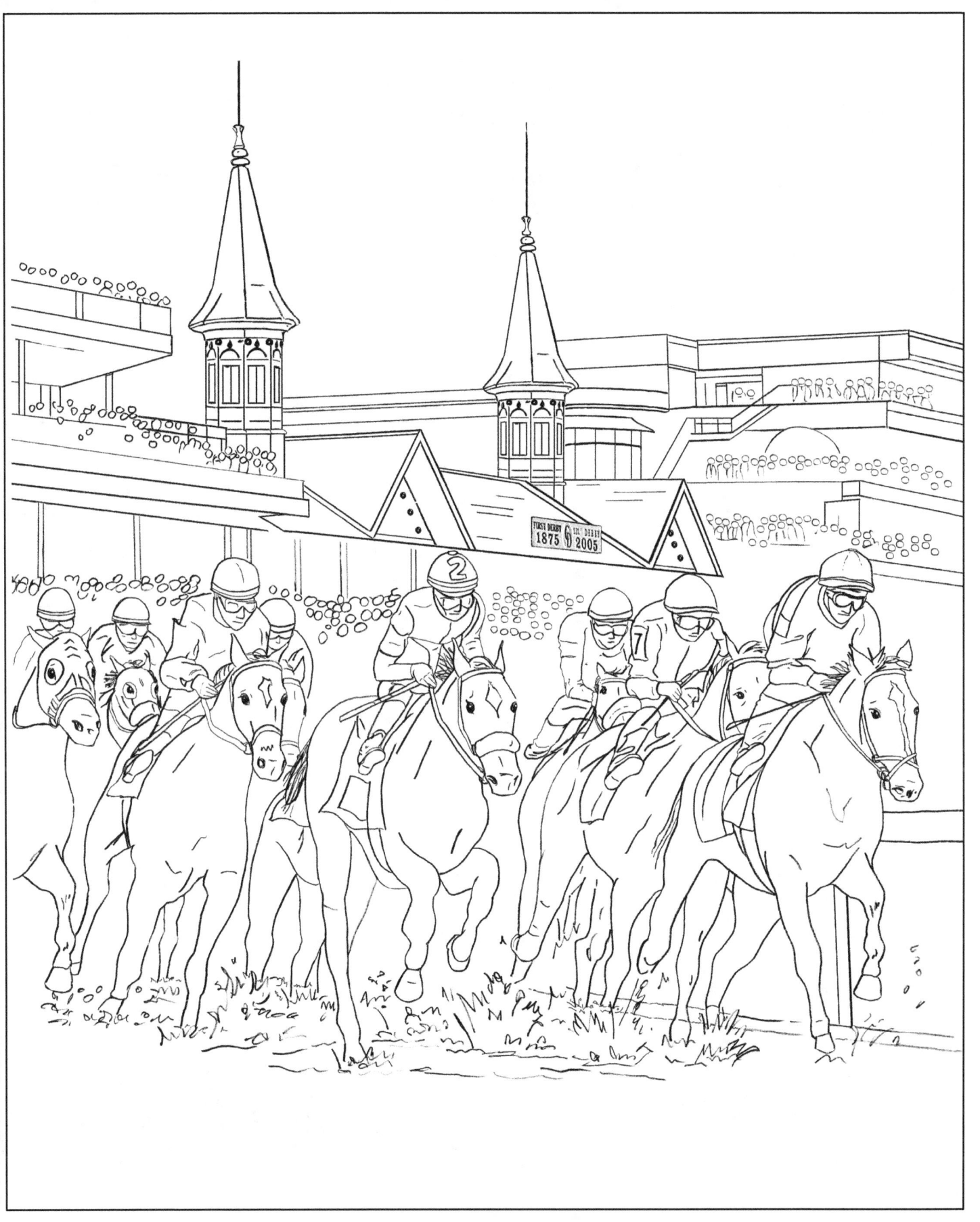

Kentucky Derby

Churchill Downs ★ Louisville

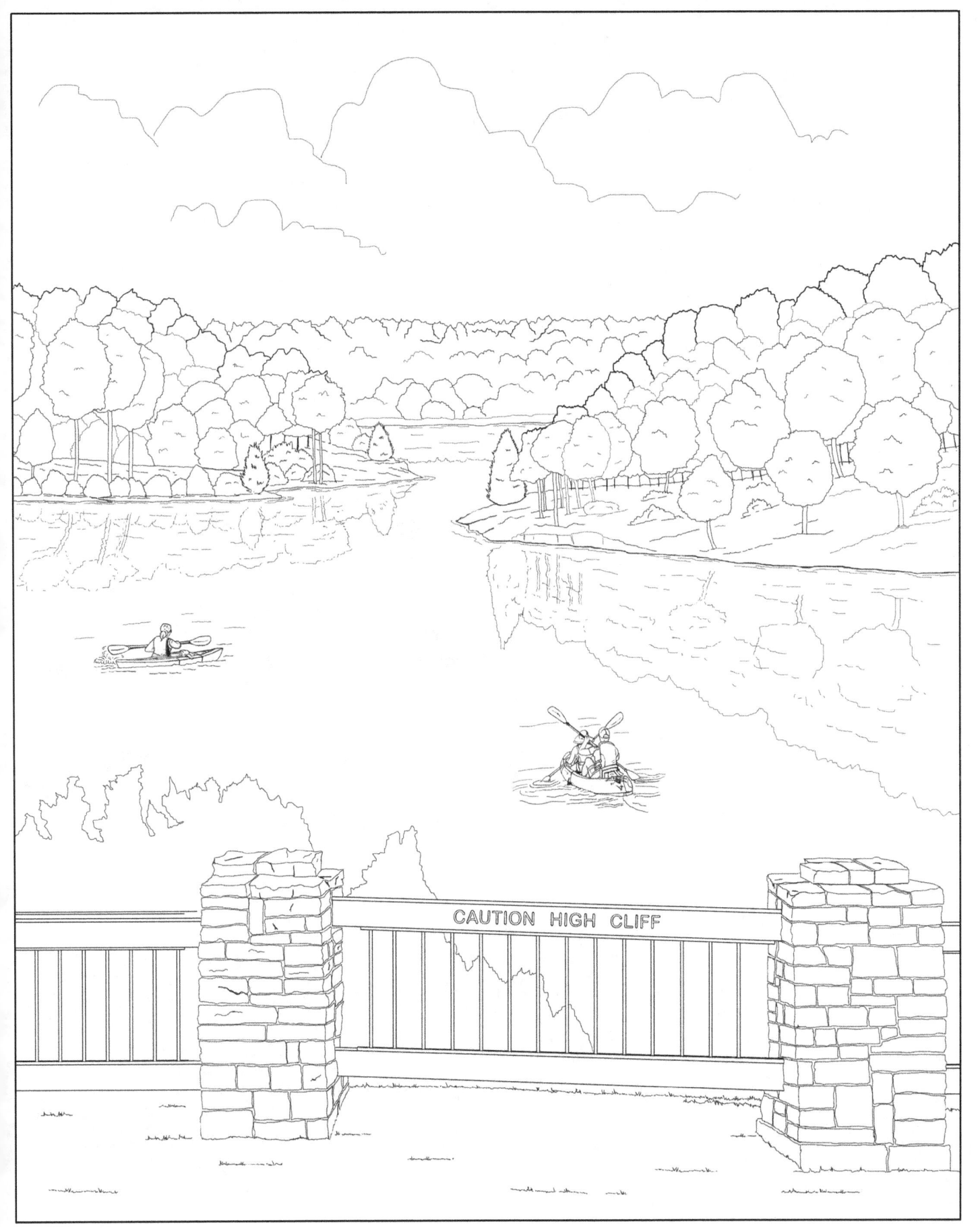

CAUTION HIGH CLIFF

Pennyrile Forest State Park

Pennyrile Lake ★ Dawson Springs

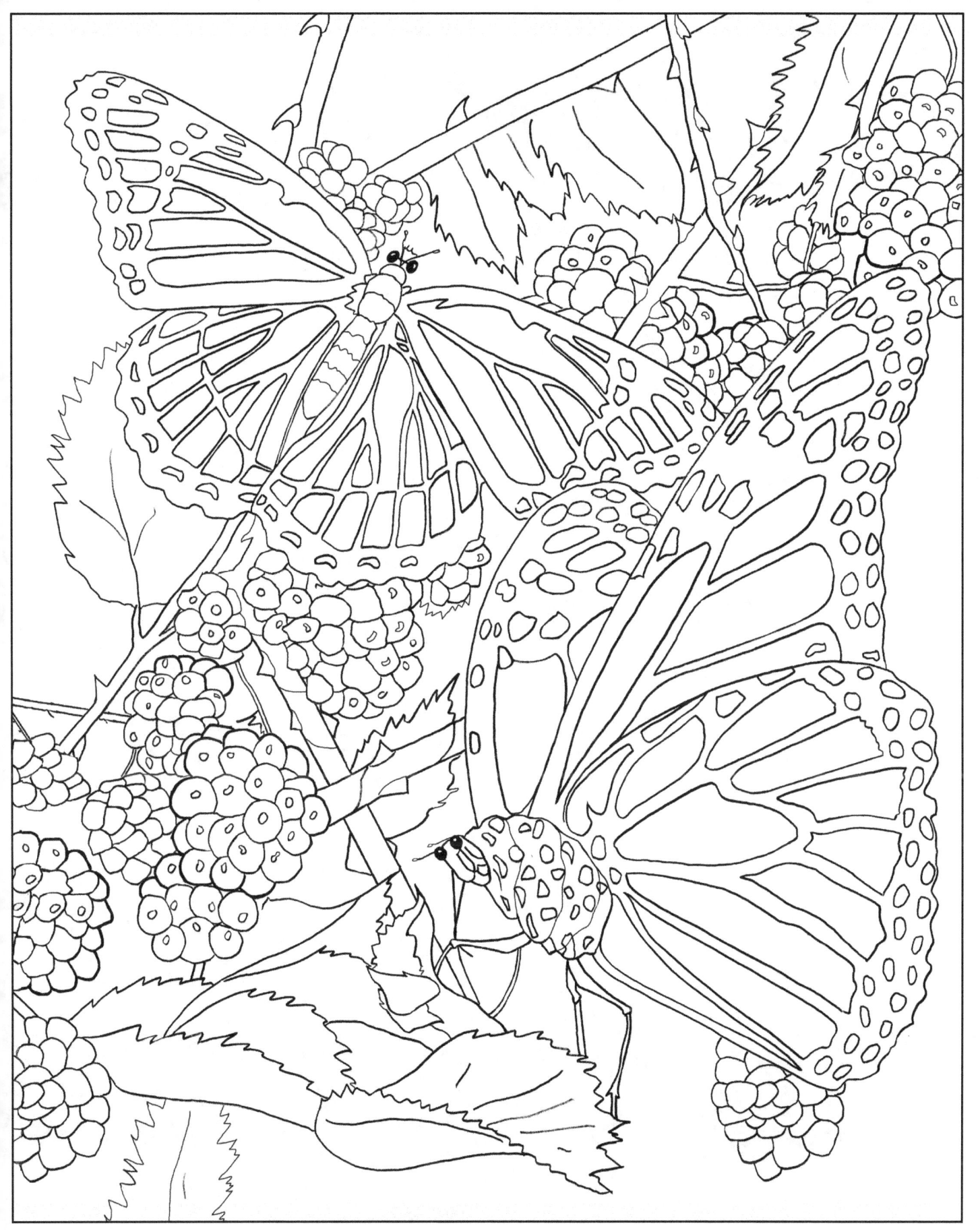

Blackberries & Butterflies

State Fruit is Blackberry ★ State Butterfly is the Viceroy

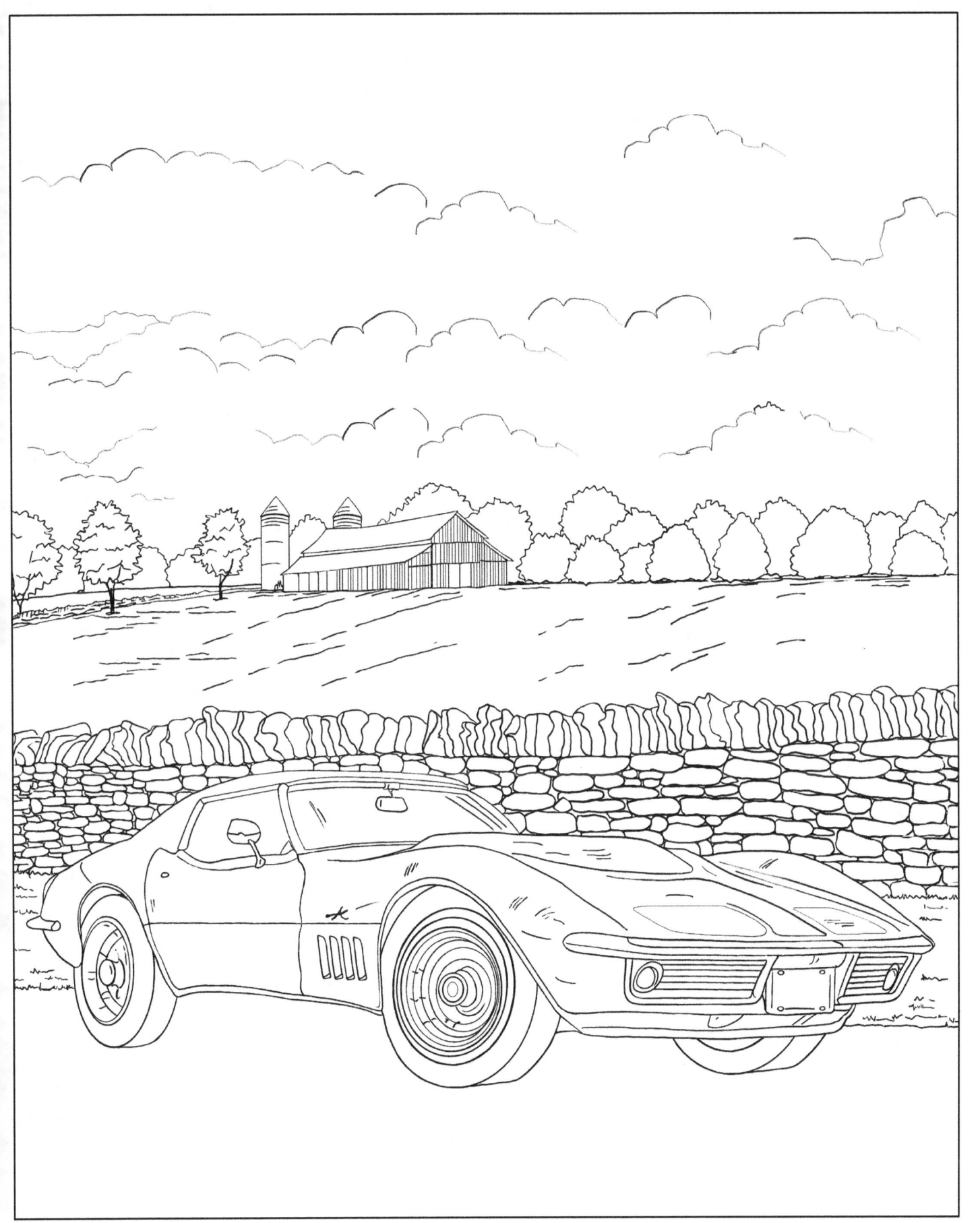

Corvette

State sports car ★ Stone fences of the Bluegrass

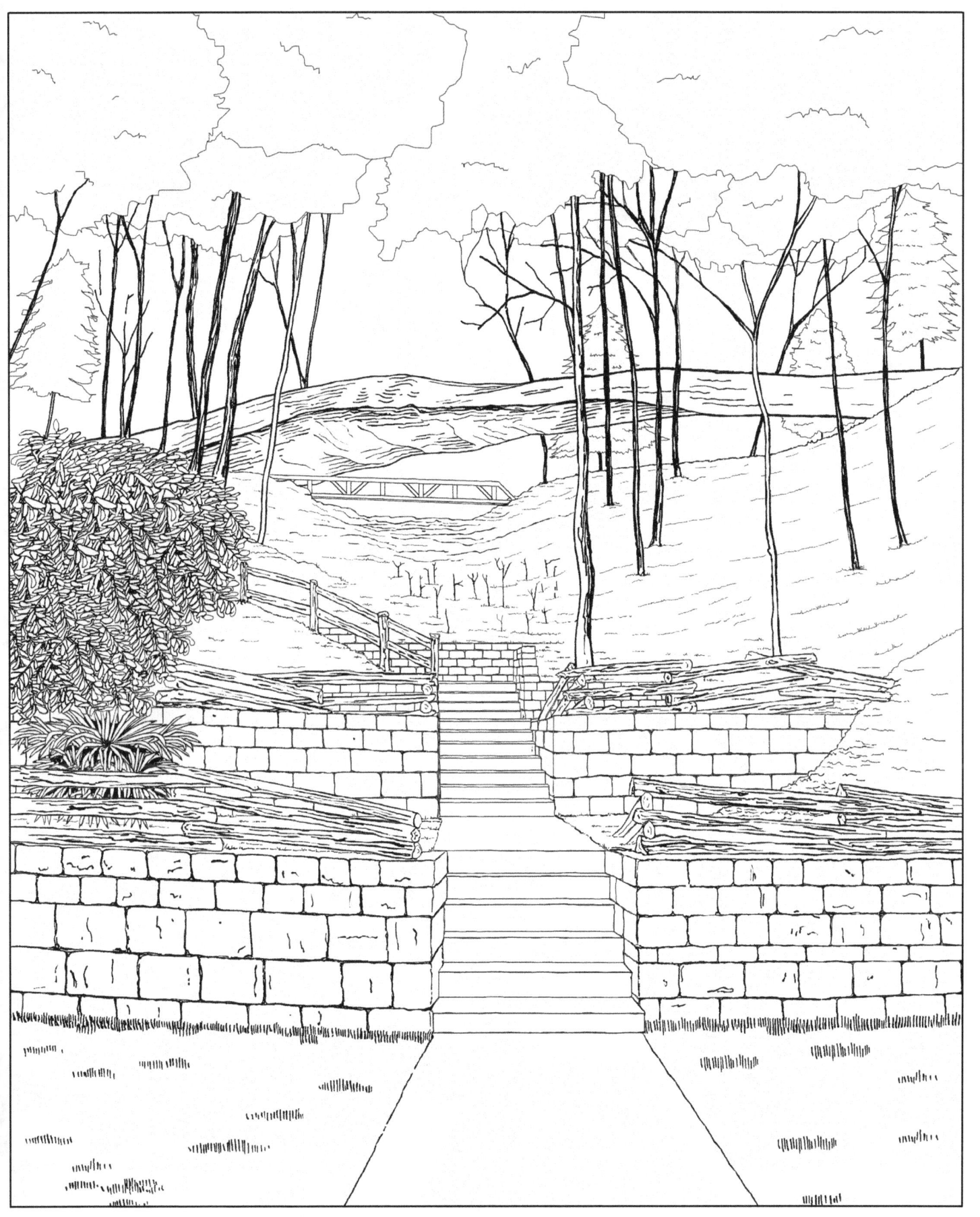

Log Rock

Kingdom Come Park ★ Harlan County

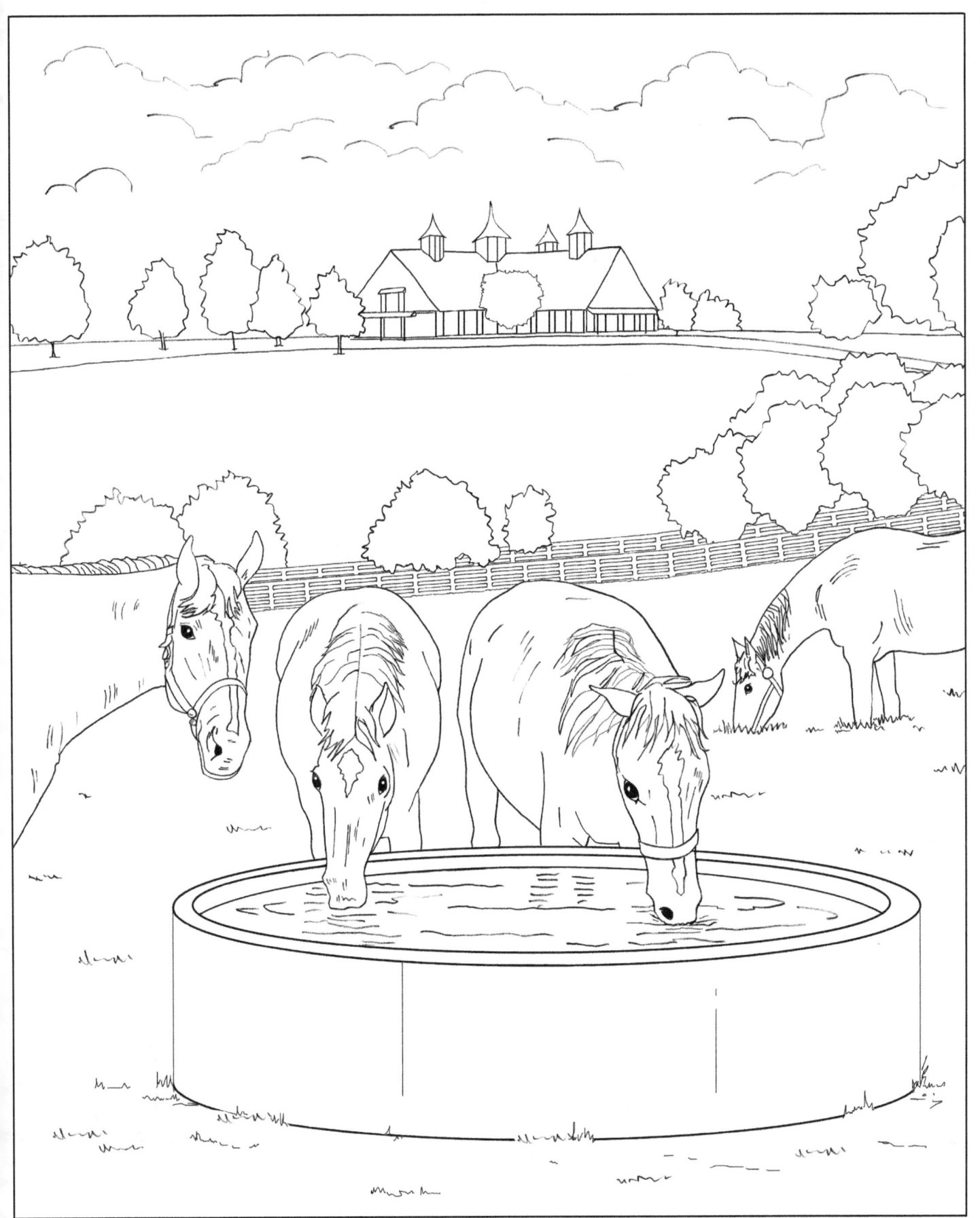

Thoroughbred Horses

State horse of Kentucky

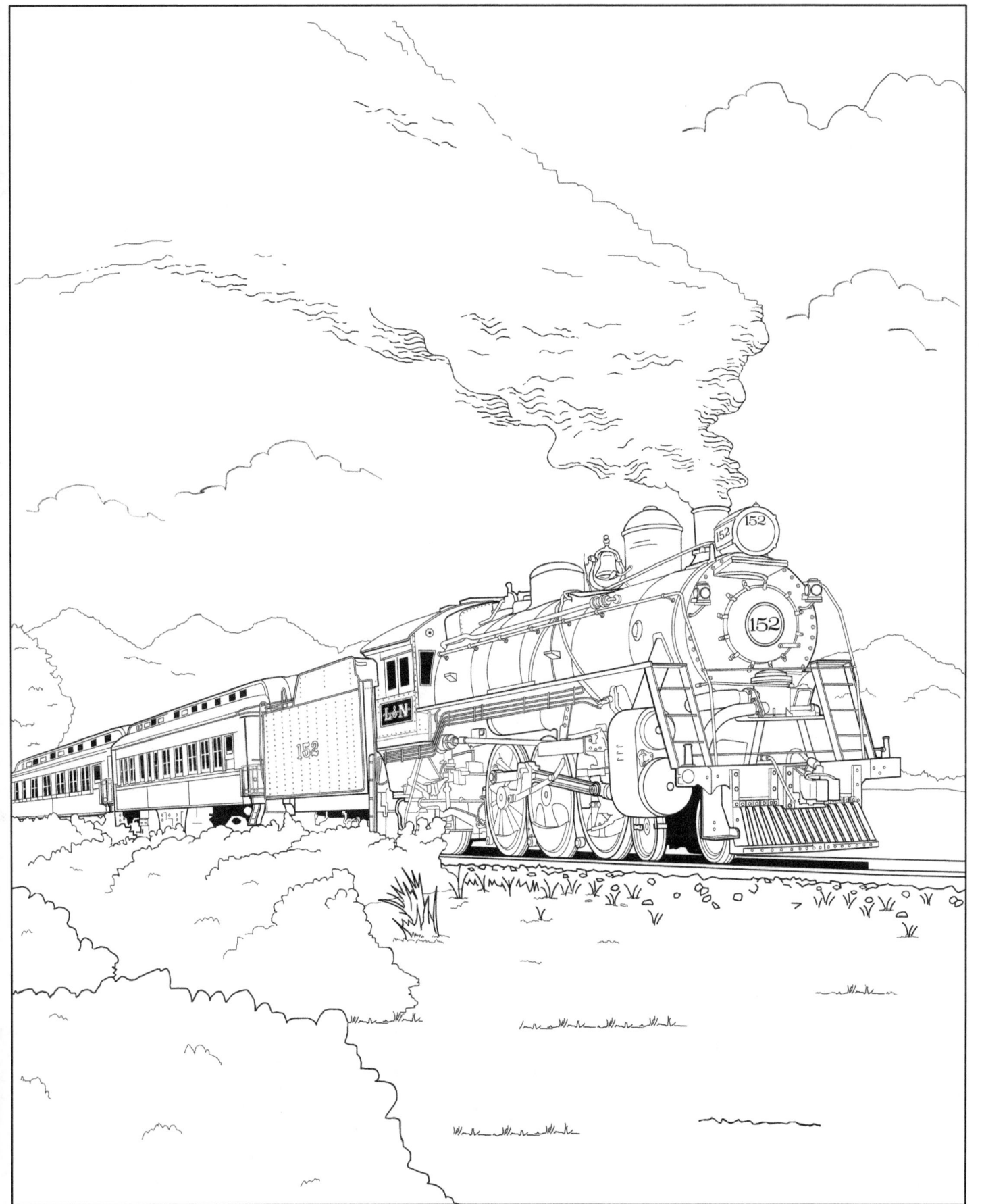

L & N # *152*

Kentucky Railway Museum ★ New Haven

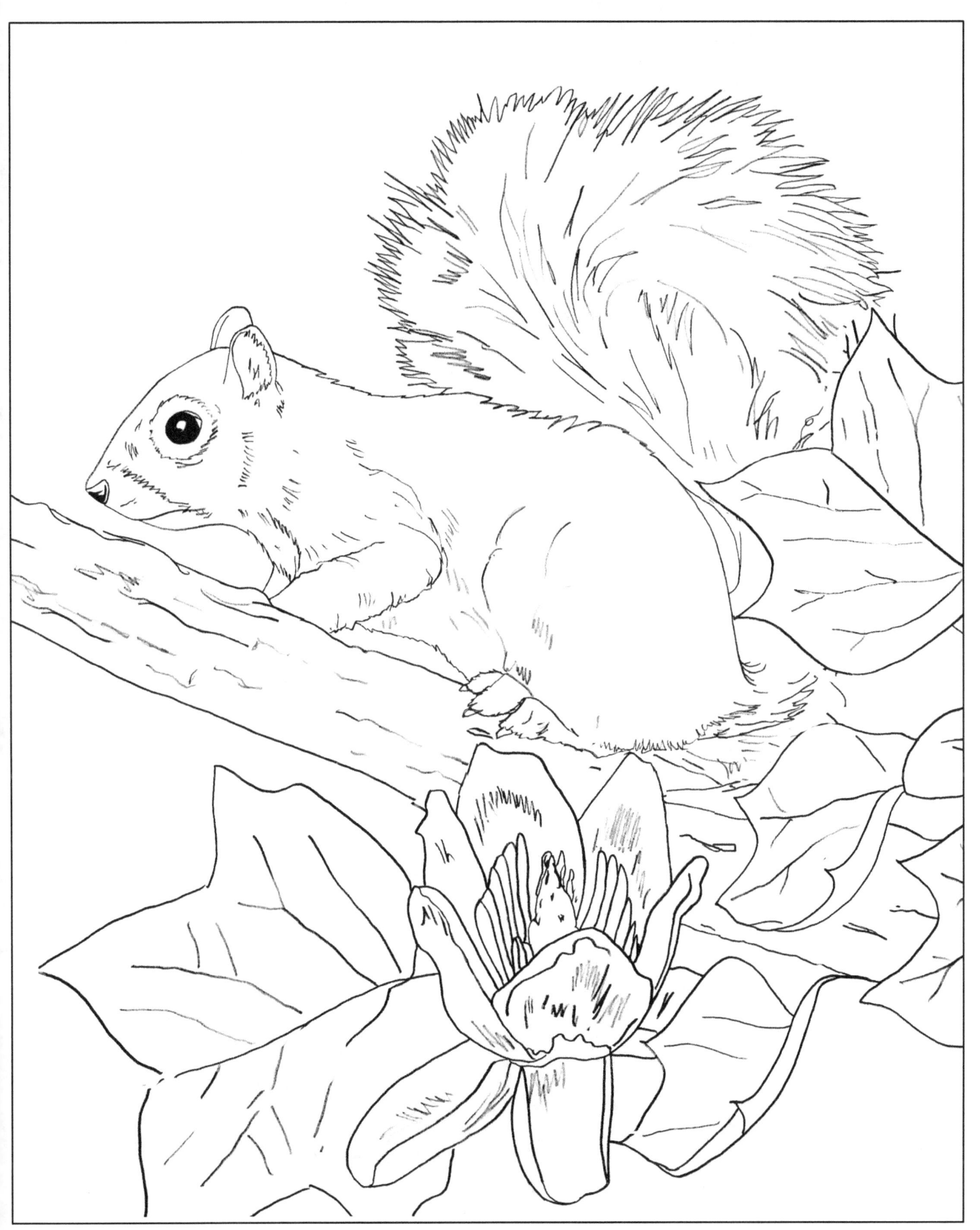

Gray Squirrel On Tulip Poplar

State wild animal and State tree

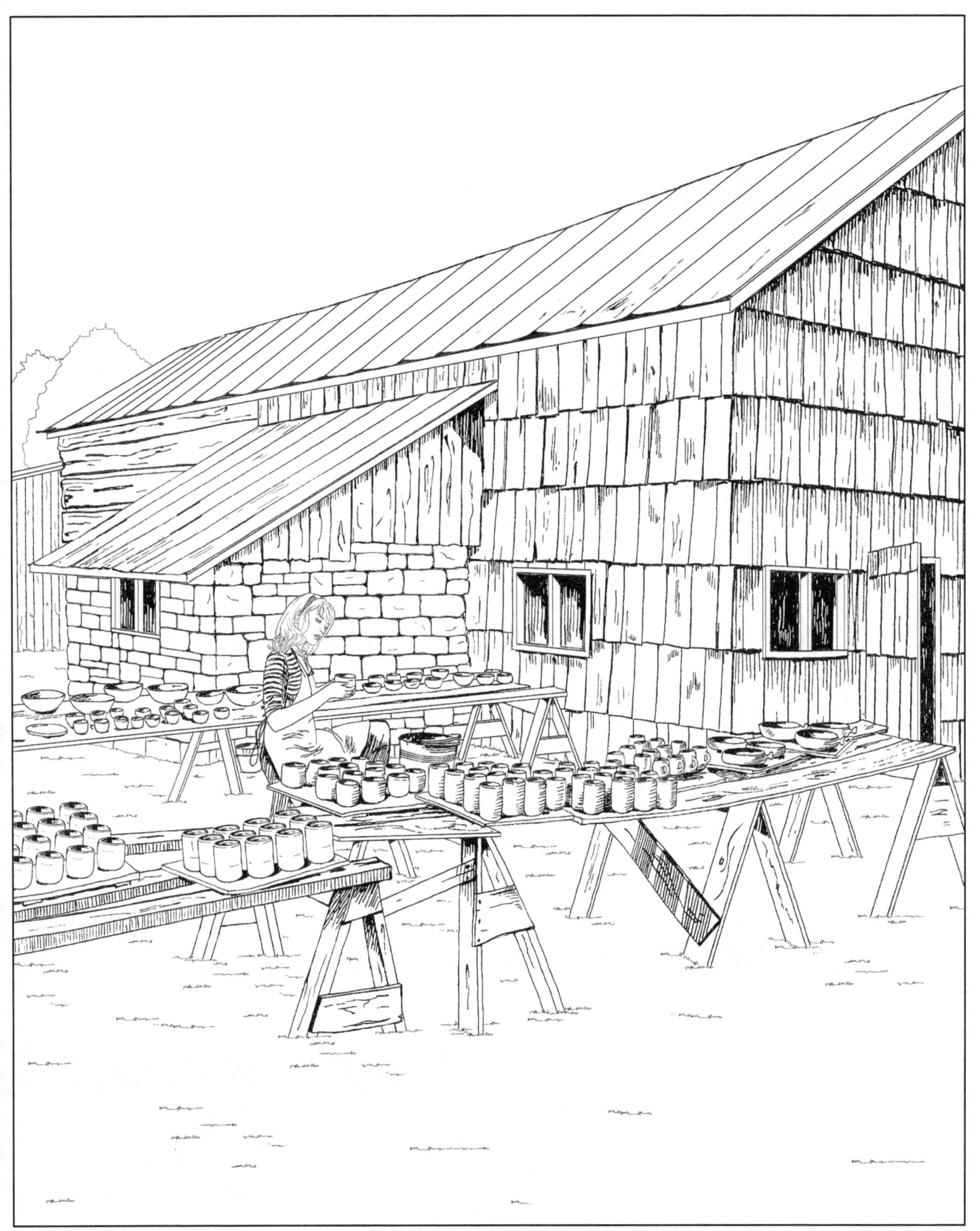

Bybee Pottery

Bybee ★ Madison County

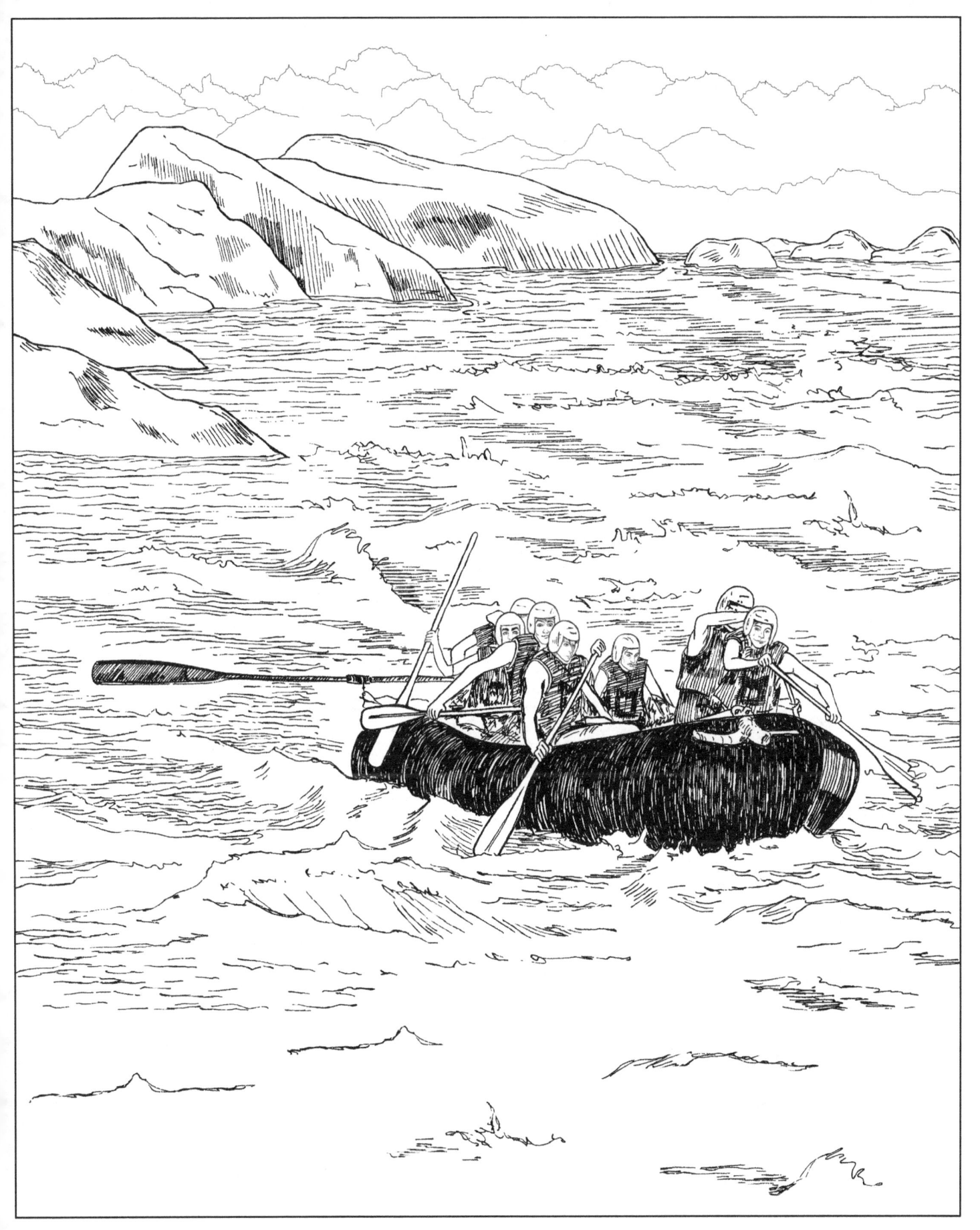

Kentucky Whitewater Rafting

Elkhorn City ★ Pike County

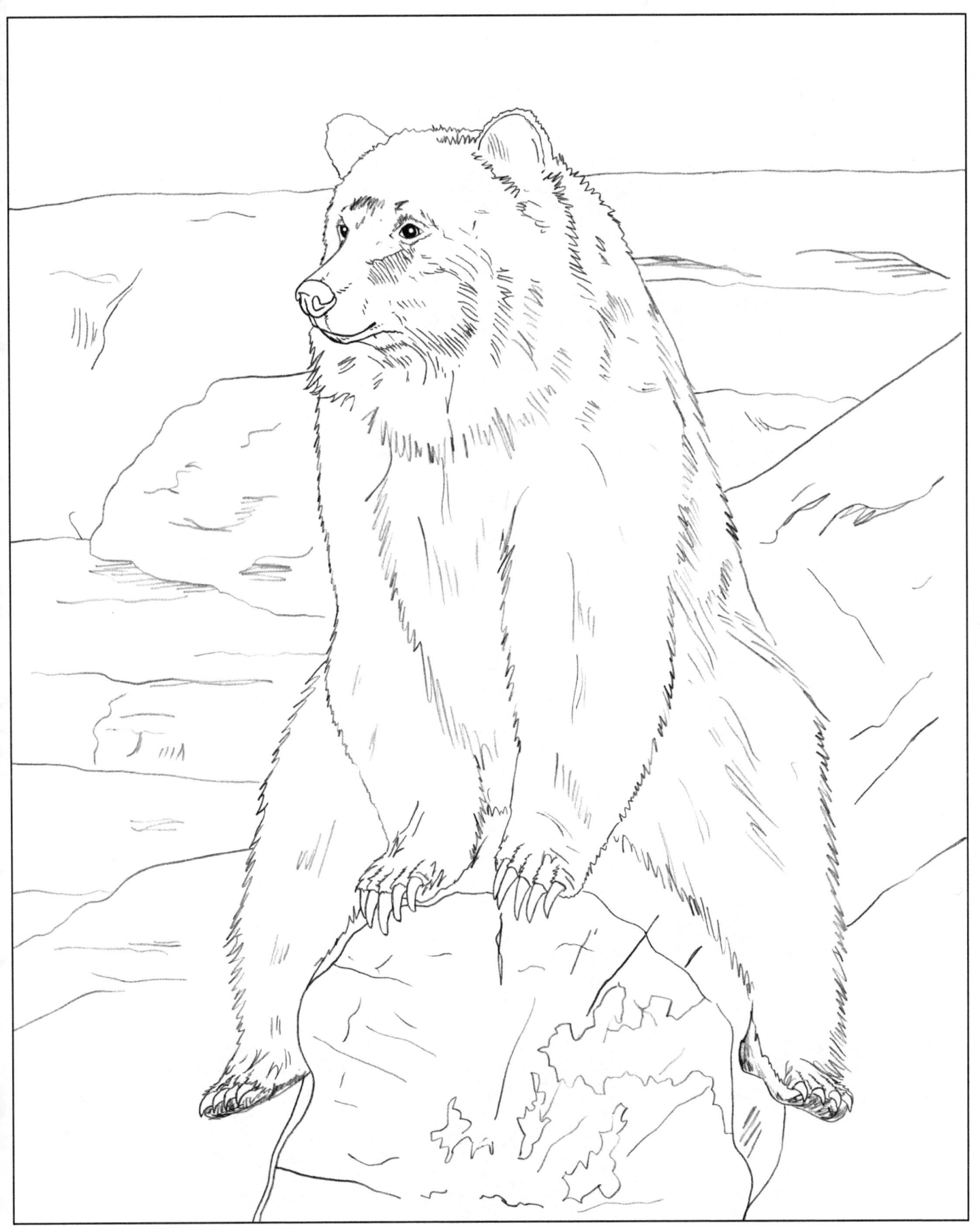

Black Bear

Eastern Kentucky

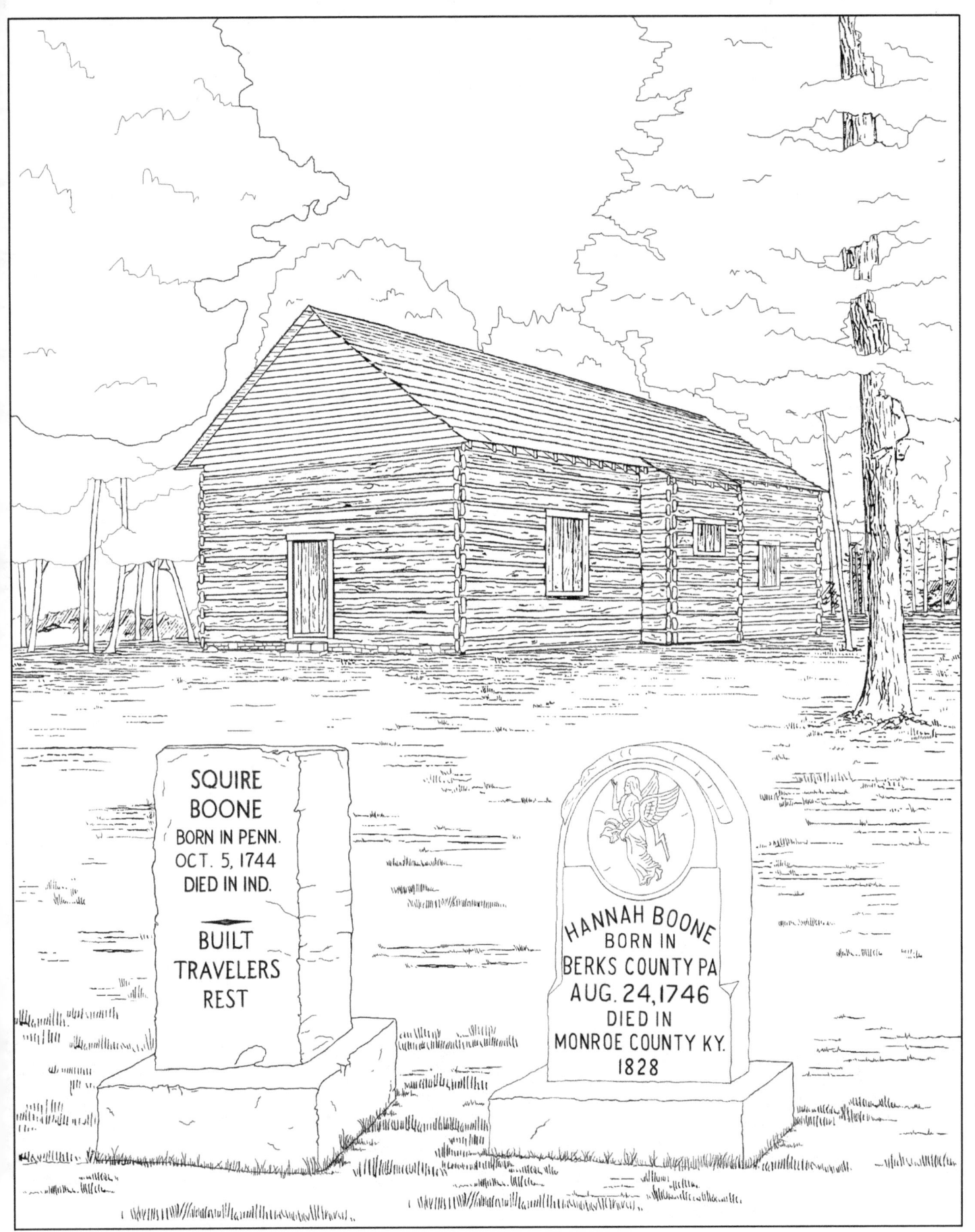

Old Mulkey Meetinghouse

Tompkinsville ★ Monroe County

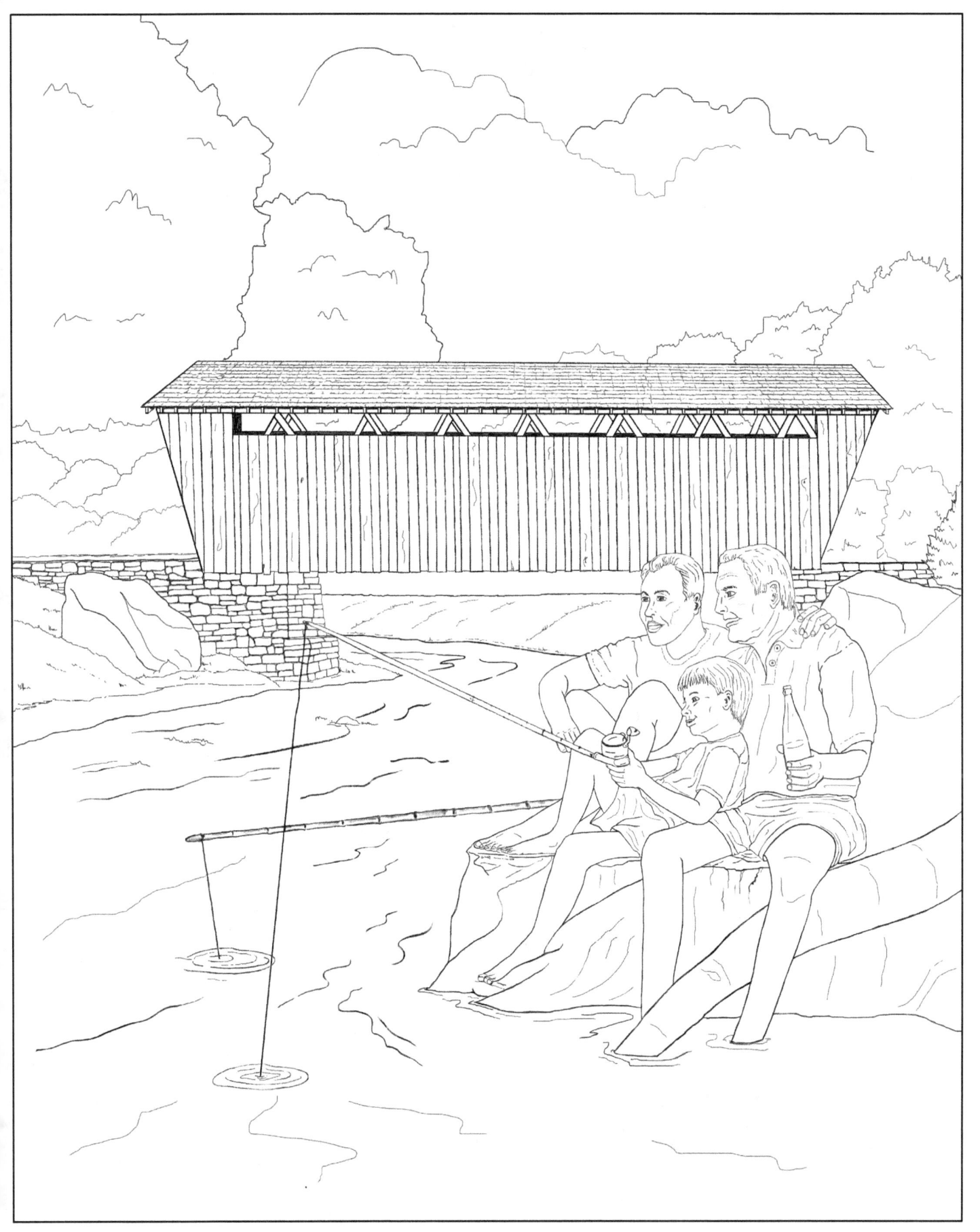

Switzer Covered Bridge

State covered bridge ★ Franklin County

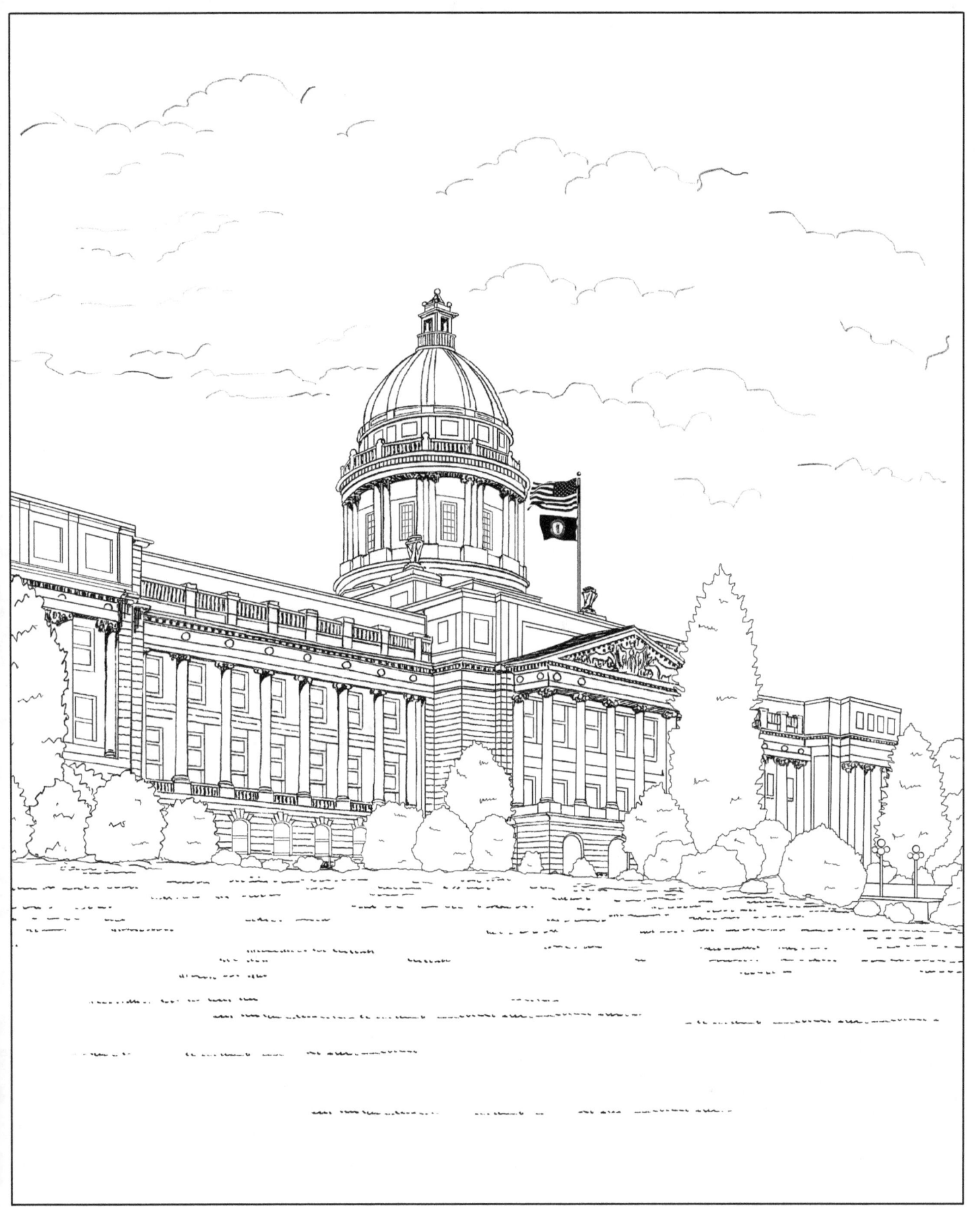

Kentucky Capitol

Frankfort ★ Franklin County

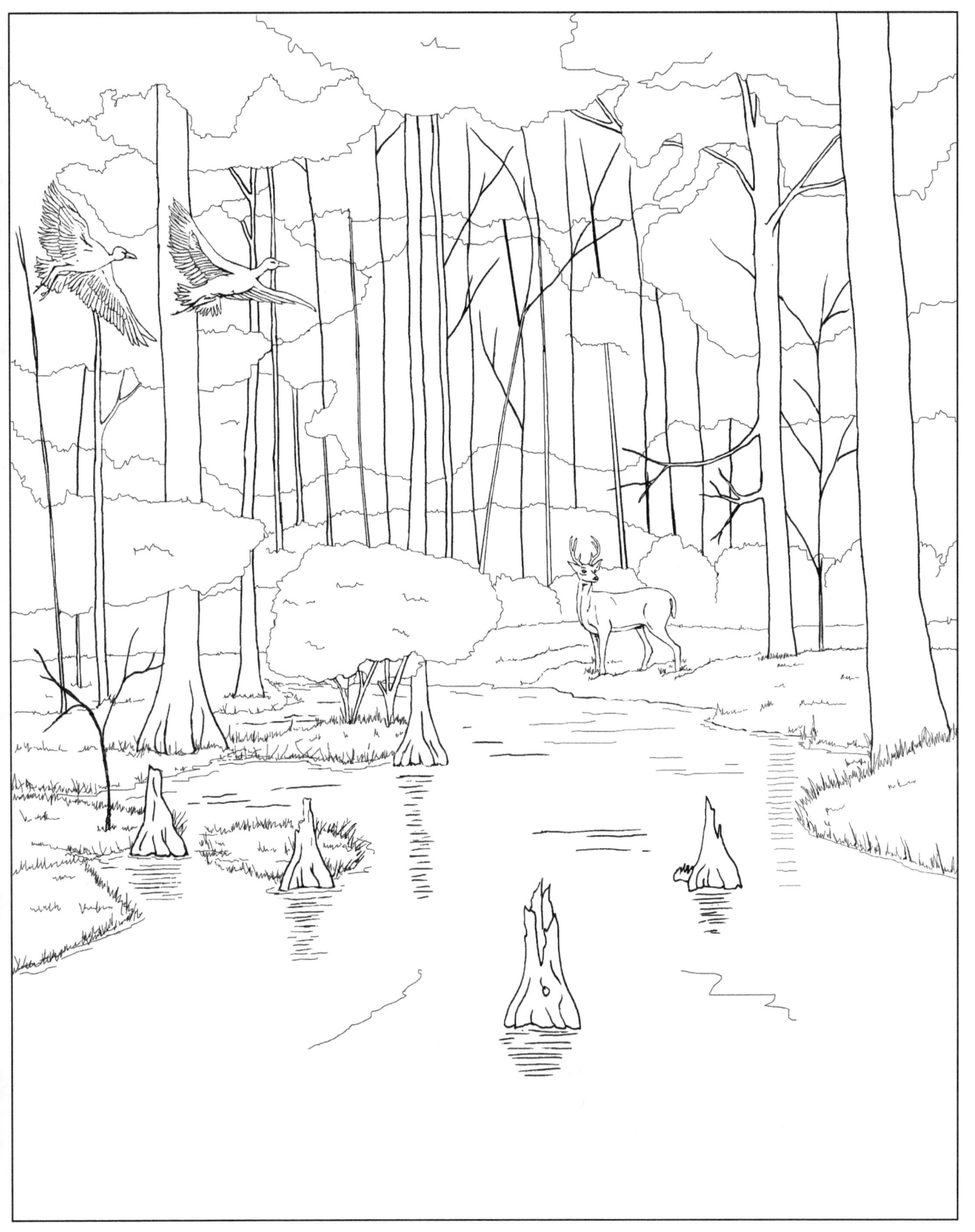

Axe Lake Swamp

Barlow Bottoms ★ Ballard County

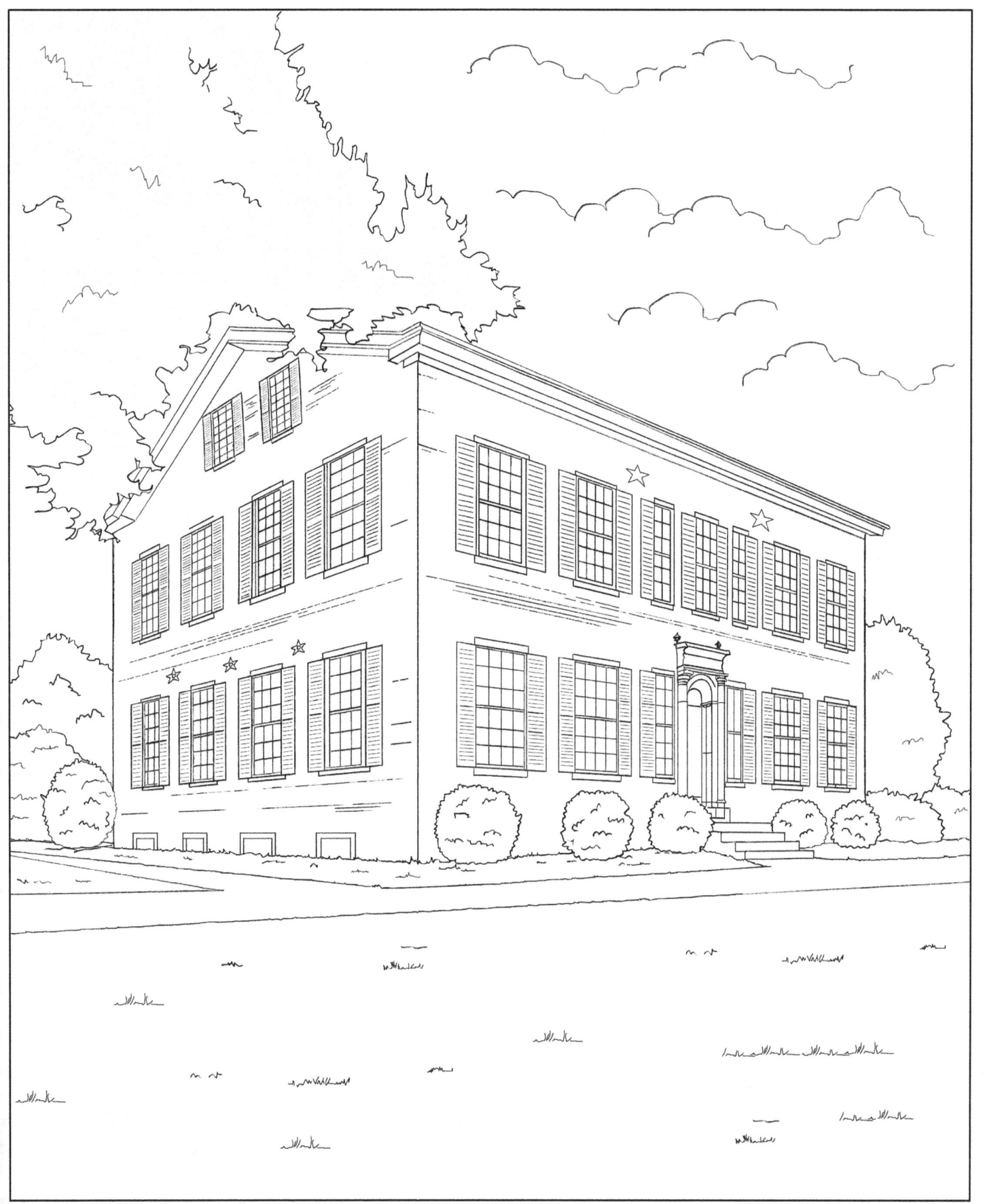

My Old Kentucky Home

Bardstown ★ Nelson County

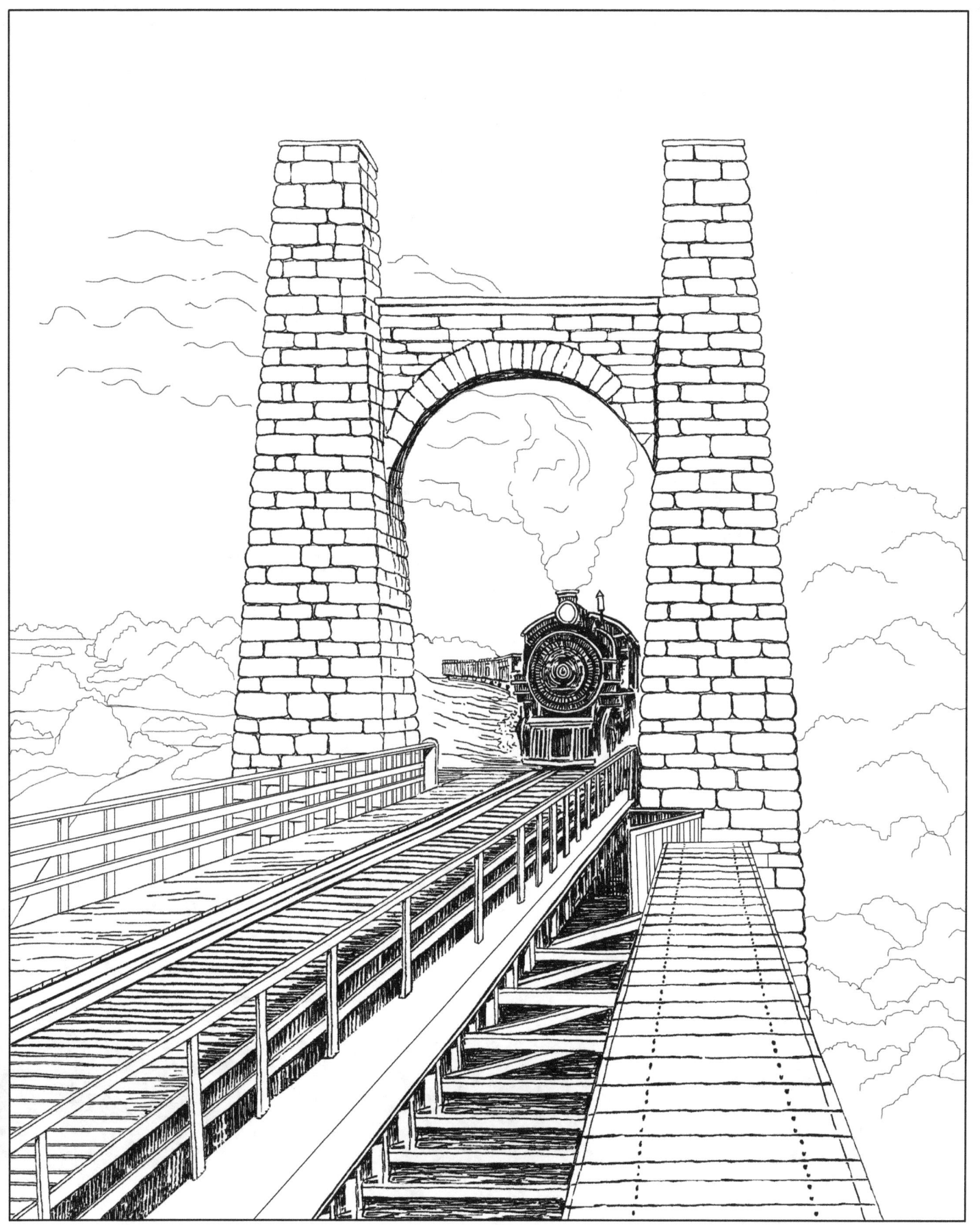

High Bridge

Over the Kentucky River ★ Jessamine-Mercer counties

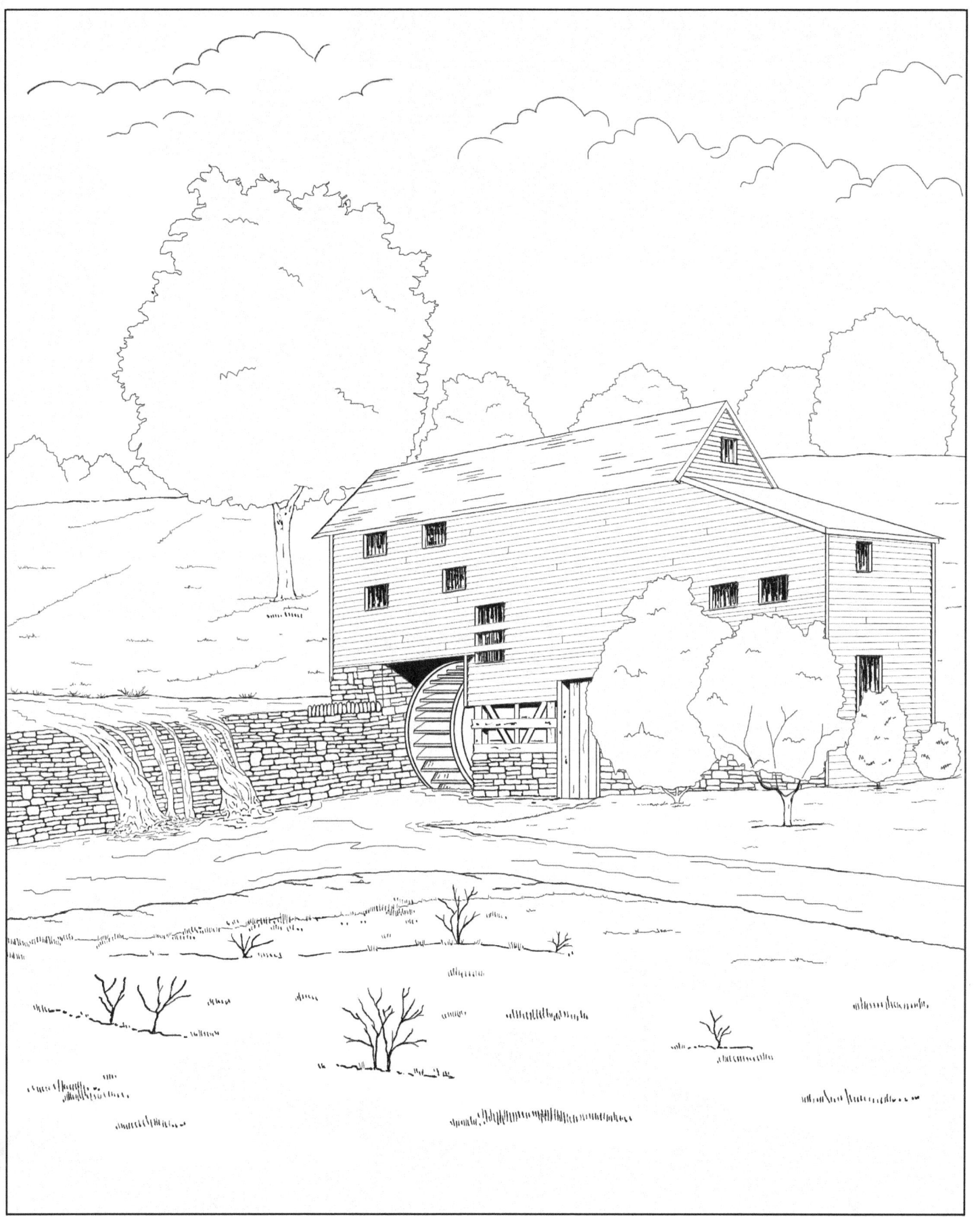

Ryman's Mill

South Elkhorn Creek ★ Fayette County

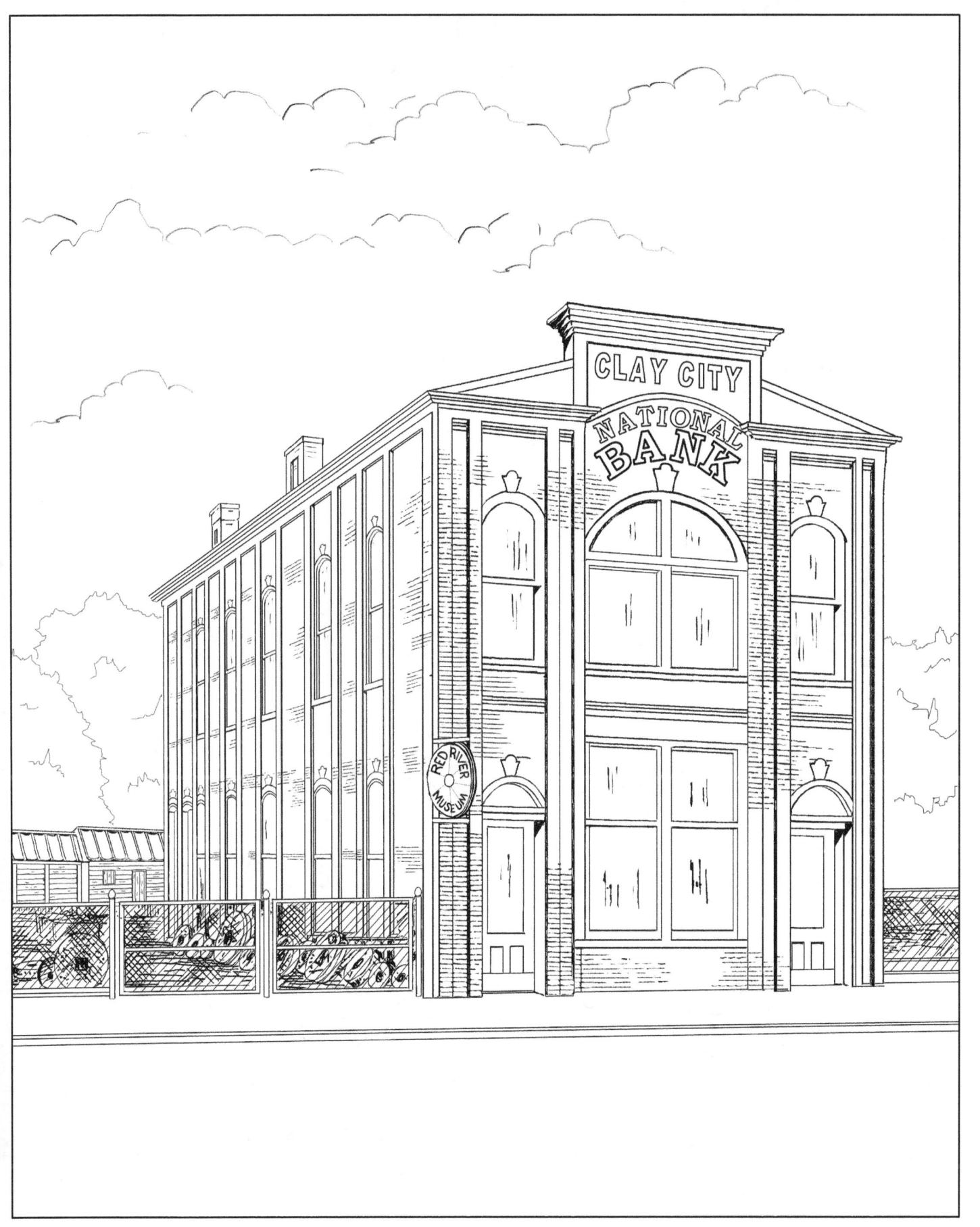

Red River Museum

Clay City ★ Powell County

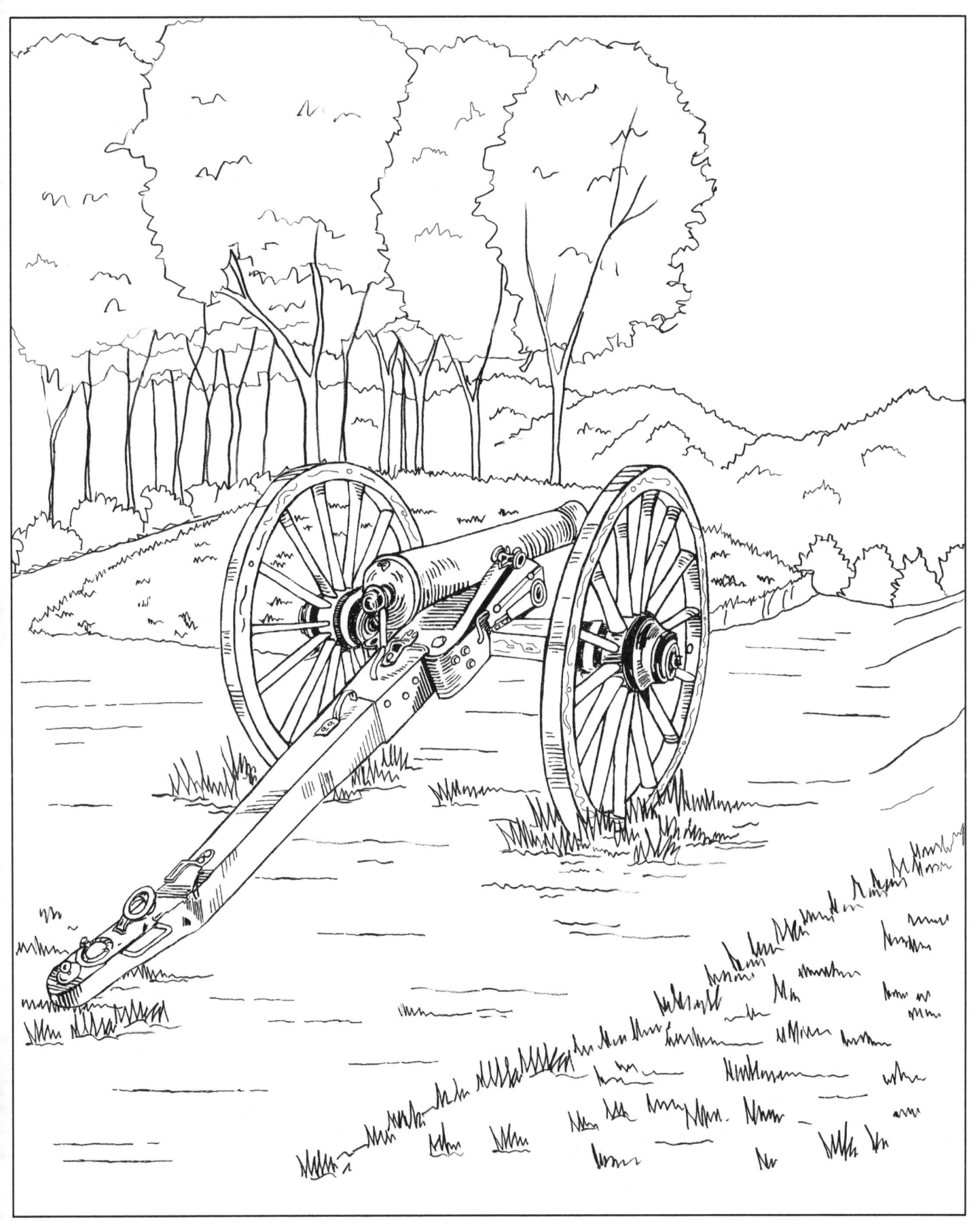

Cannon at Cumberland Gap

Cumberland Gap ★ Middlesboro/ Bell County

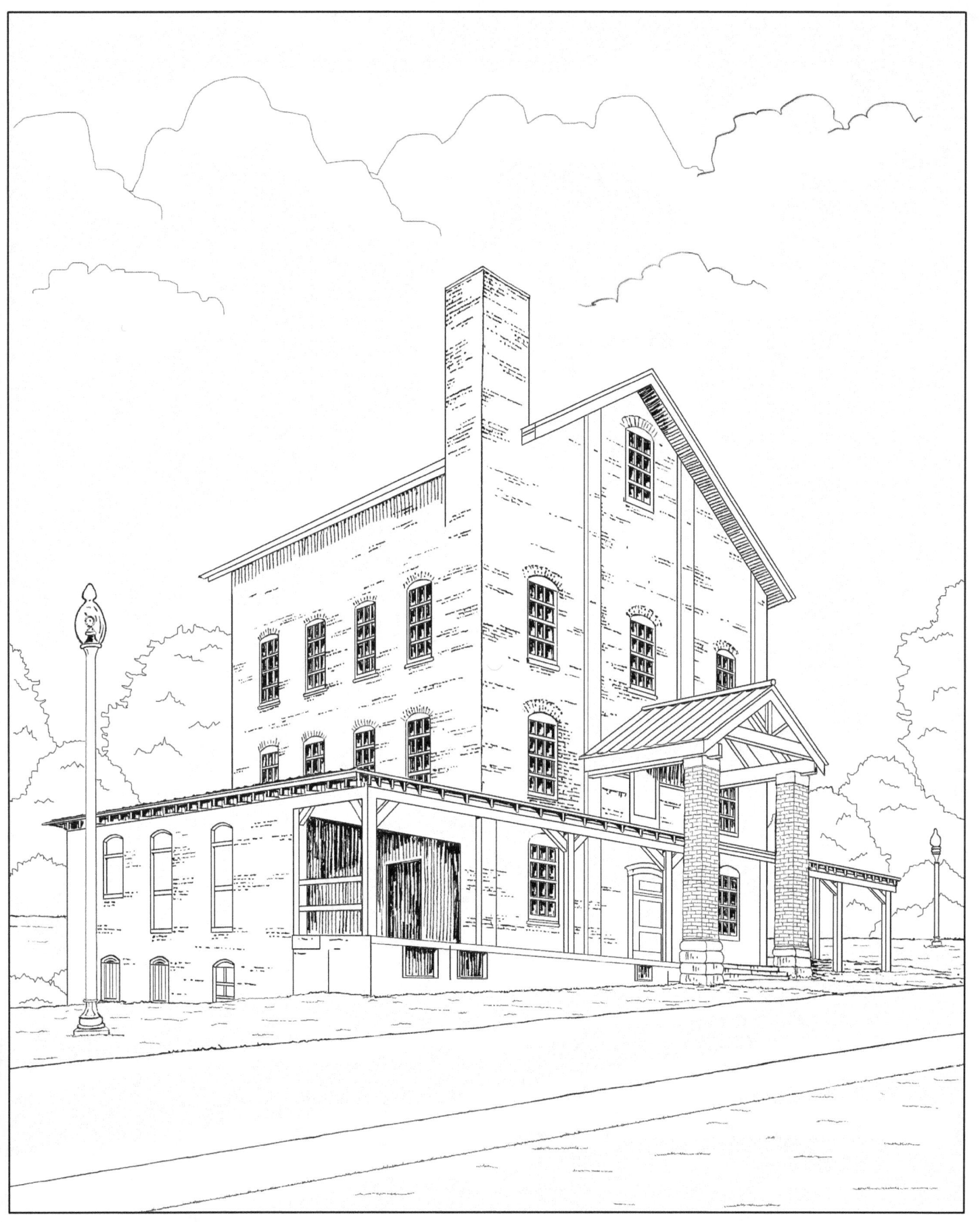

Baughman Mill

Stanford ★ Lincoln County

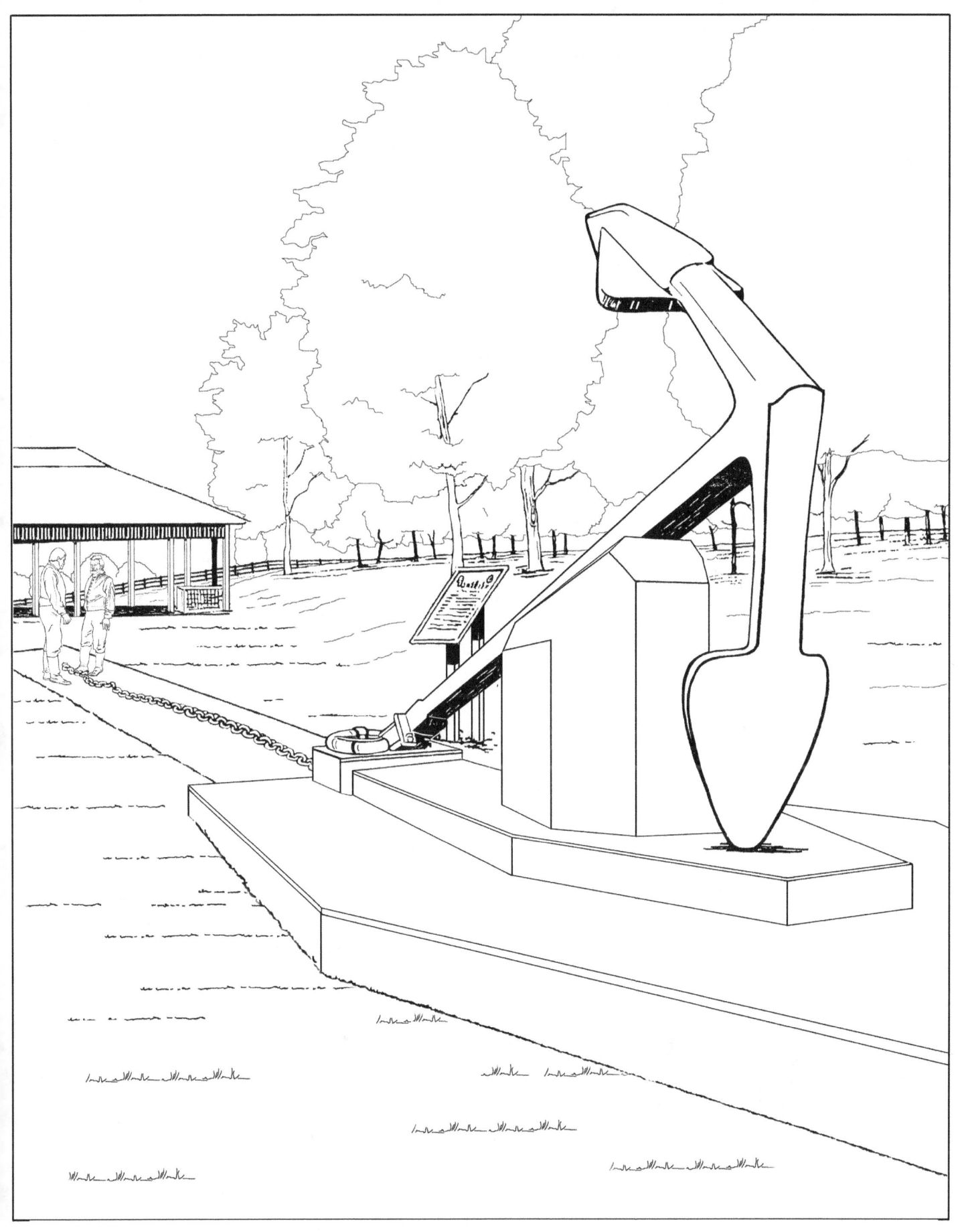

Columbus–Belmont Battlefield

Civil War Park ★ Hickman County

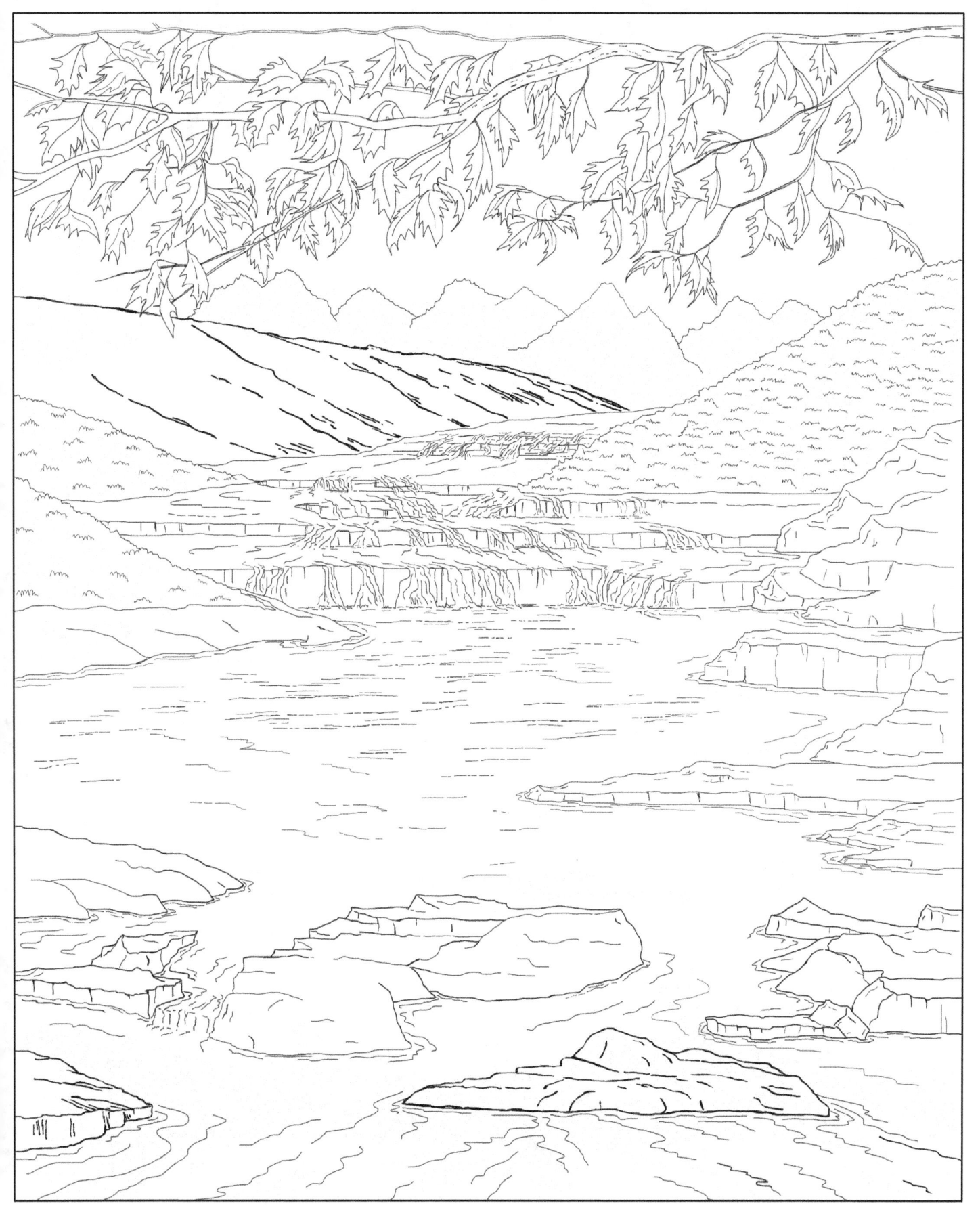

Raven Run Nature Preserve

Lexington ★ Fayette County

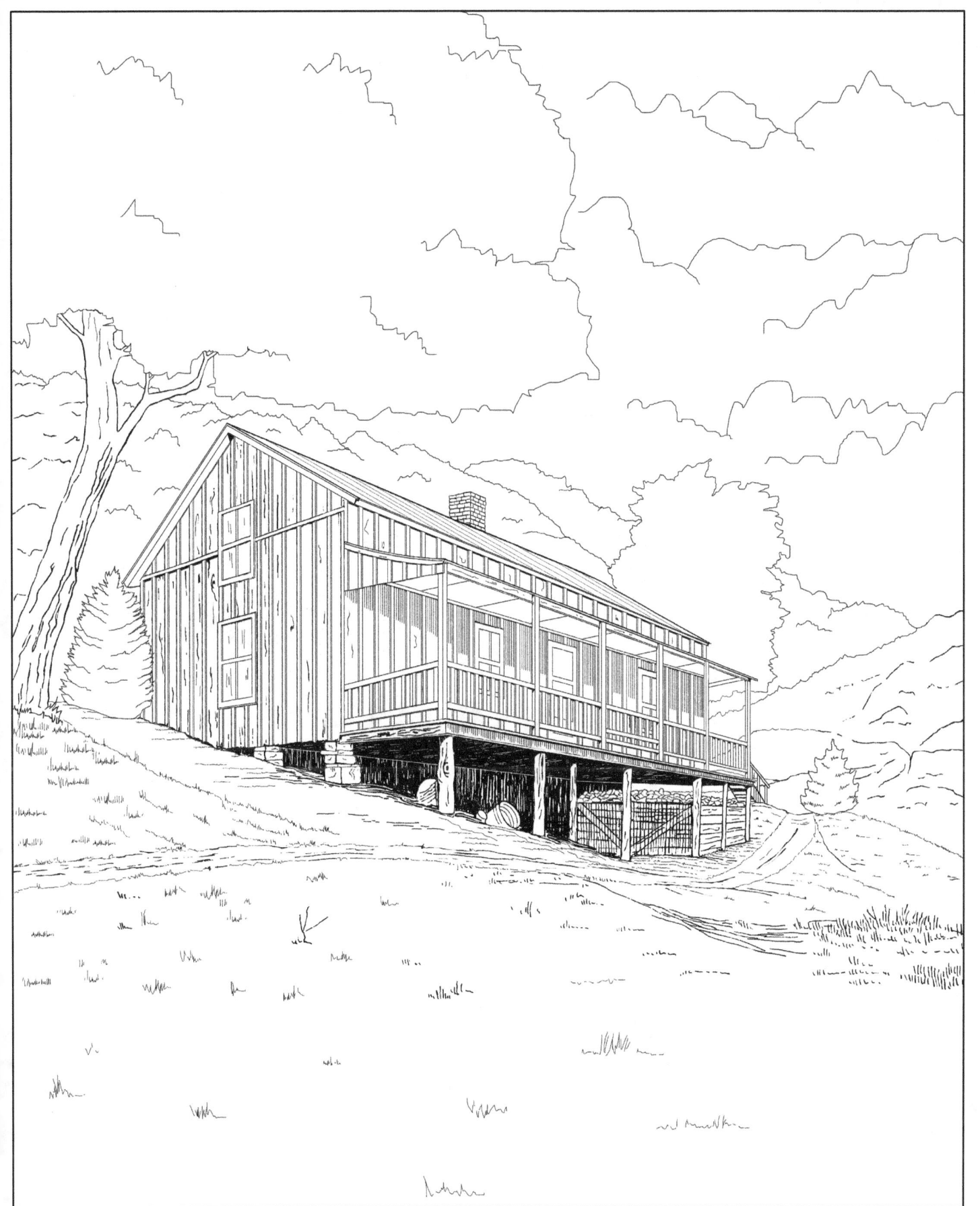

Butcher Hollow

Loretta Lynn's Home ★ Van Lear/ Johnson County

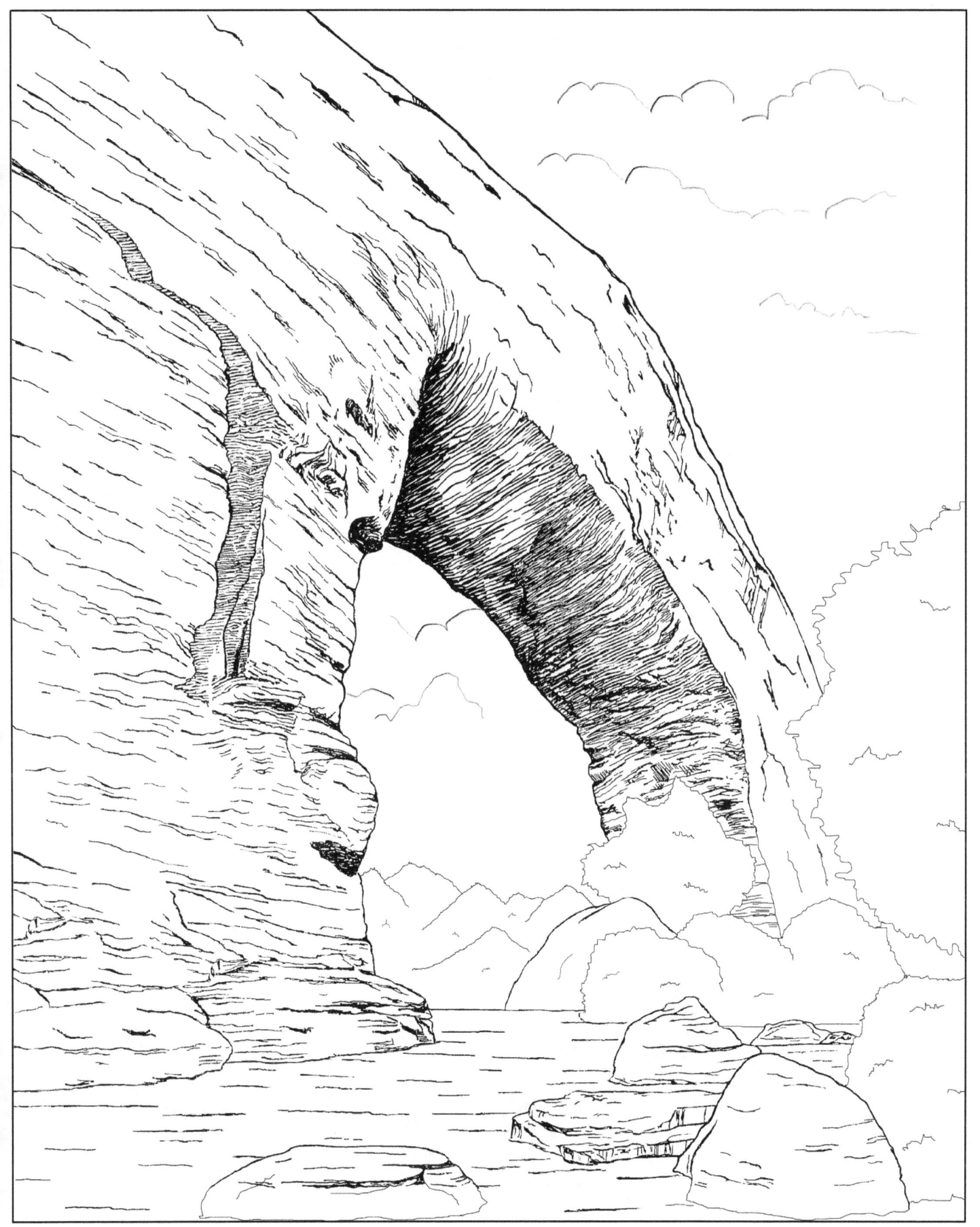

Natural Bridge

Slade ★ Powell County

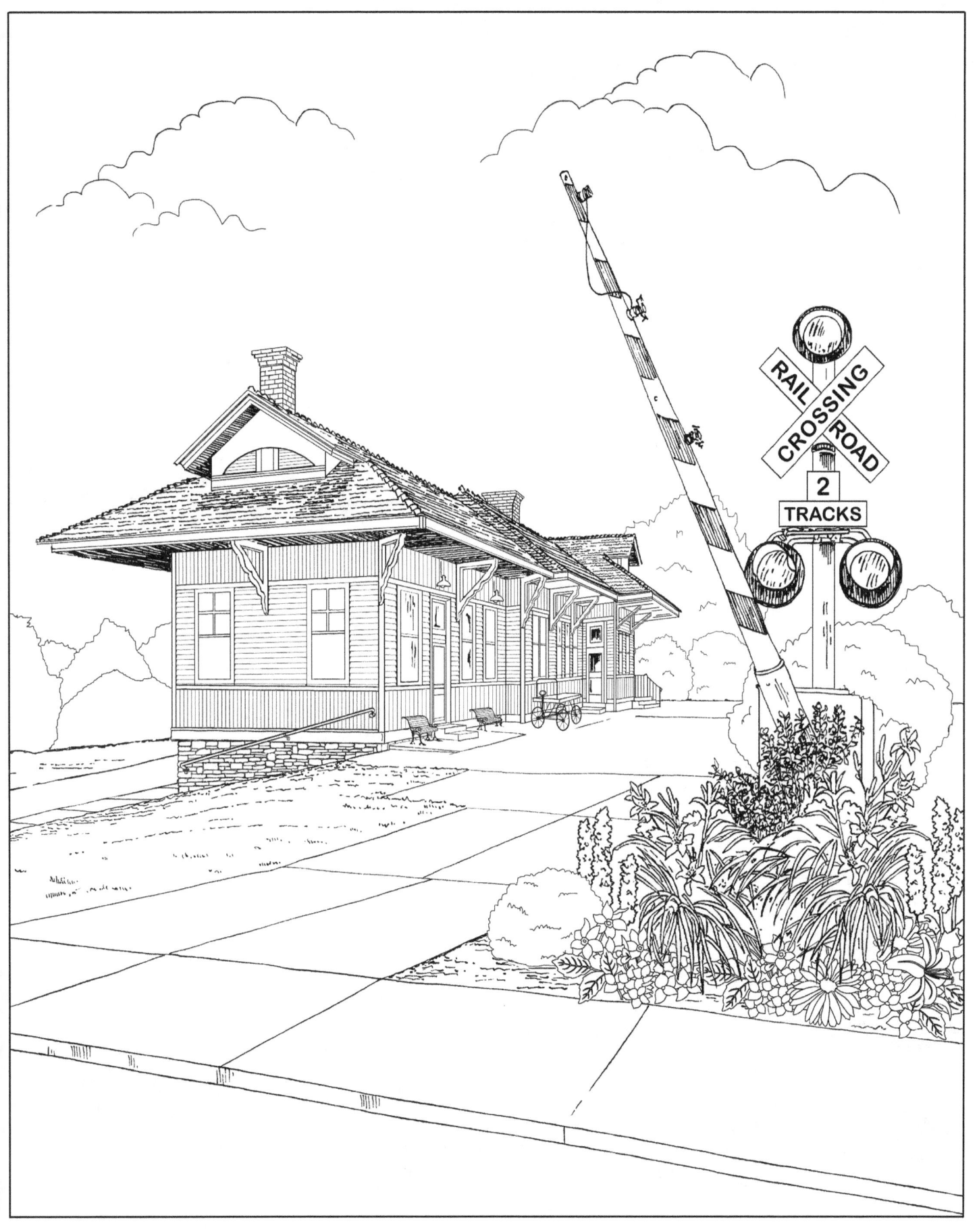

L & N Depot

Stanford ★ Lincoln County

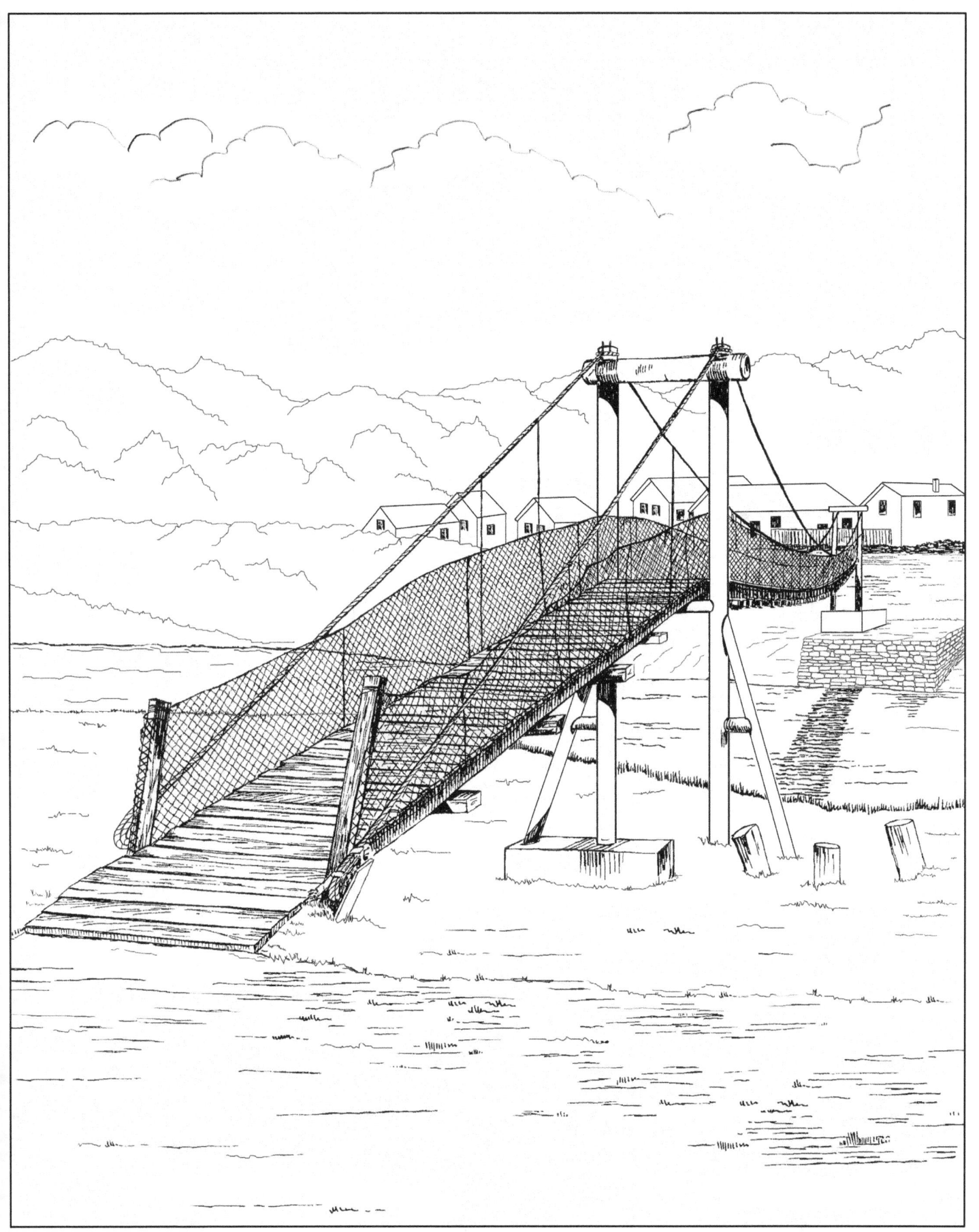

Swinging Bridge

Loyall ★ Harlan County

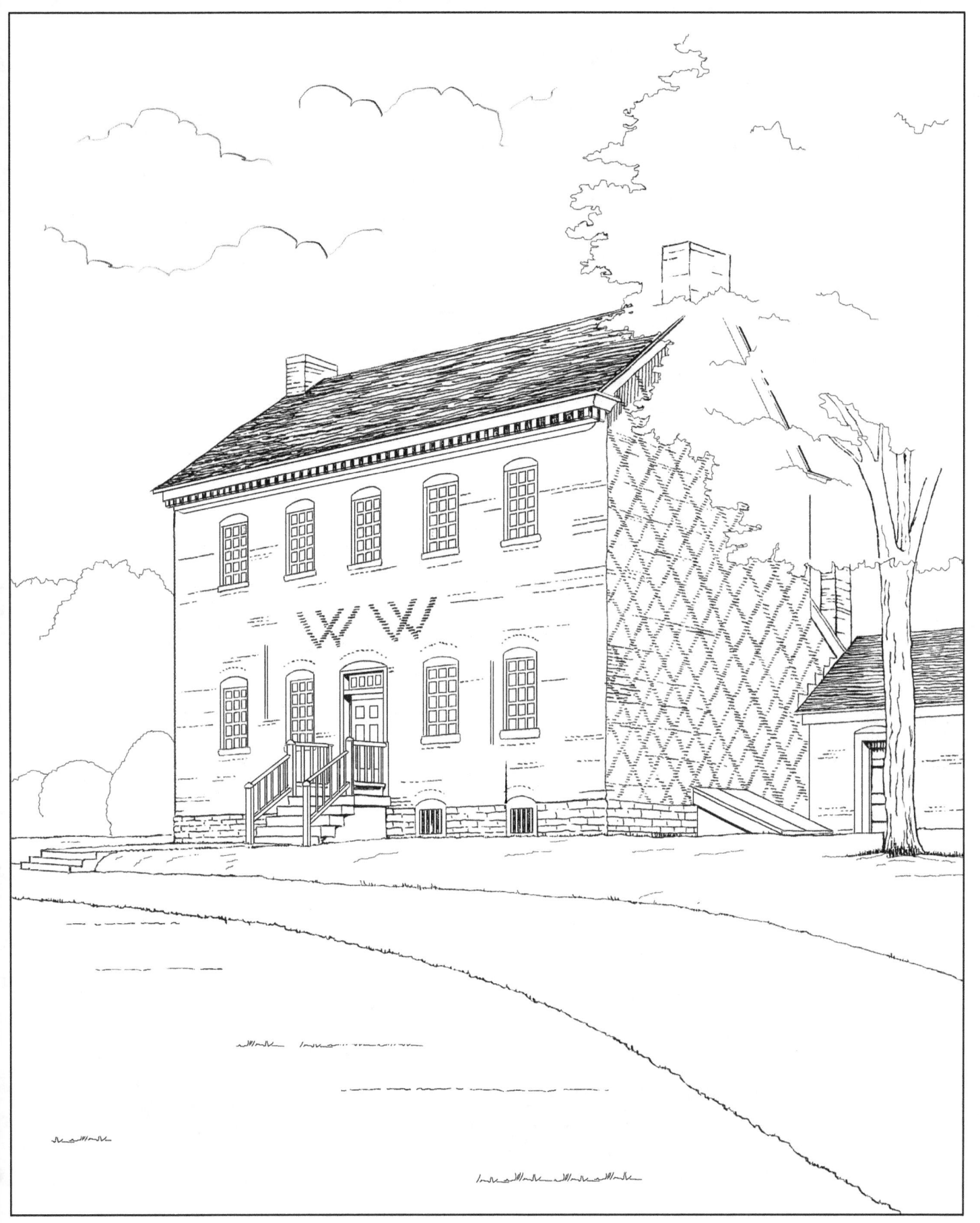

William Whitley House

Sportsman Hill ★ Lincoln County

ALPHABETICAL INDEX

Brief Subject Notes

The Angles (Paducah / McCracken County)

This home in Paducah was built by Quintus Quincy Quigley in 1853. It later became the home of Alben W. Barkley, one of the state's best-loved politicians. He was born in Graves County and was 14 when his family moved to a farm near Clinton. Barkley was admitted to the Kentucky Bar in 1902, and opened his law practice in Paducah. He was elected prosecuting attorney for McCracken County in 1905 and was then elected County Judge in 1908. Barkley acquired "The Angles" property in 1937. A consummate politician, Barkley never lost an election during his career. He was a member of the U.S. Congress from 1913 until election to the U.S. Senate in 1927. Barkley was elected Vice-President as the running mate with Harry S. Truman in 1949. He expected to succeed Truman, but at age 74 was considered too old for President by his own Democrat party.

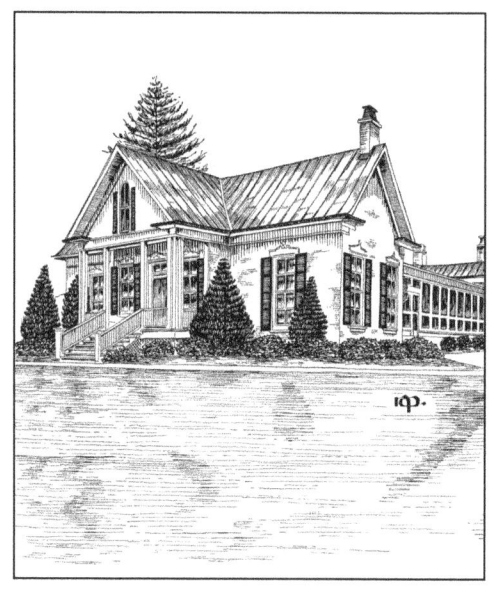

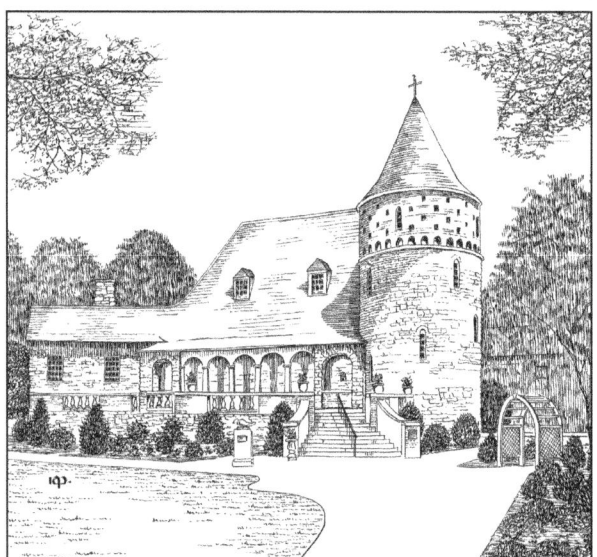

Audubon State Park (Henderson/ Henderson Co.)

is a 692-acre wildlife sanctuary donated by the citizens of Henderson, in memory of the ornithologist and artist who roamed through the state from 1808 to 1826. He lived in Henderson for several years, gathering material for his monumental *Birds of America*. The park includes Audubon's favorite haunts. In the "French Garden" is a small pavilion and two birdbaths, which are formed from old millstones found on the site of his "infernal mill." The French Norman architecture style was chosen because of his French ancestry, and it permits the round tower on the museum that contains numerous holes for nesting birds.

Aunt Polly House (Renfro Valley/ Rockcastle County)

Located across Hummel Road from the Renfro Valley complex, this is now the *Aunt Polly House Gift Shop*. It is one of the numerous fascinating attractions in this miraculous valley designed to preserve the concept of the pioneer American spirit. This old log house built around 1800 by Col. William Fish. It was moved to Renfro Valley and restored to its original condition. John Lair wanted this place to serve as a home for *Renfro Valley County Music Hall of Fame*, which he expected to open to the public in 1975. However, it holds a unique gift shop that is a favorite to visitors, and the Hall of Fame is in a much larger facility designed specifically for that purpose. Aunt Polly offers Kentucky Crafts, quilts, molasses, honey, jams, homemade fudge, hand-dipped ice cream, clocks, woodcrafts, candles, baskets, ceramics, soaps, music, artwork, T-shirts, and many more items.

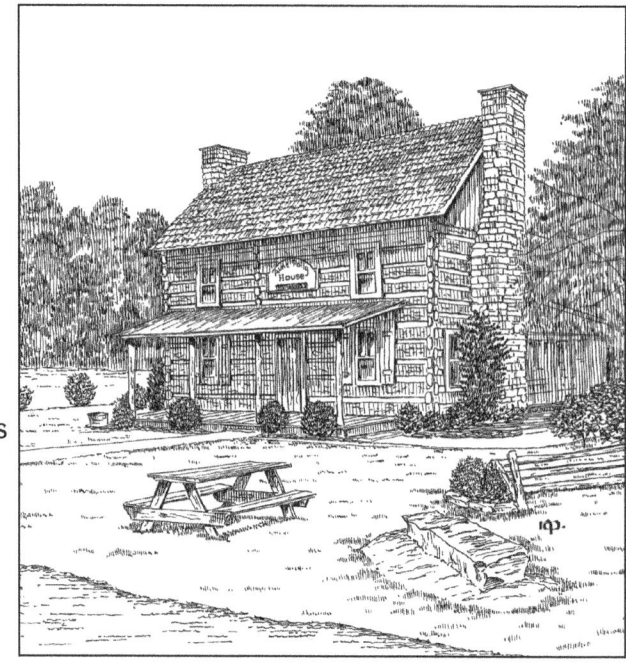

Axe Lake Swamp (Ballard County) is the rare bald cypress swamp in far-western Kentucky that was originally dedicated in 1991 as the *Axe Lake Swamp State Nature Preserve*. An additional 312 acres were dedicated in 2001 to increase the preserve to 458 acres. The land was acquired with assistance from The Kentucky Heritage Land Conservation Fund and Nature Conservancy. It was the first step toward the long-term protection of the entire 3,000-acre Axe Lake Swamp wetlands. The complex supports rare plant and animal species and contains the state's most significant nesting population of Brown Creepers. It is also utilized by large numbers of migratory waterfowl and has been recognized as a high priority wetland in the North American Waterfowl Management Plan. It supports rare plant and animal species, and waterfowl.

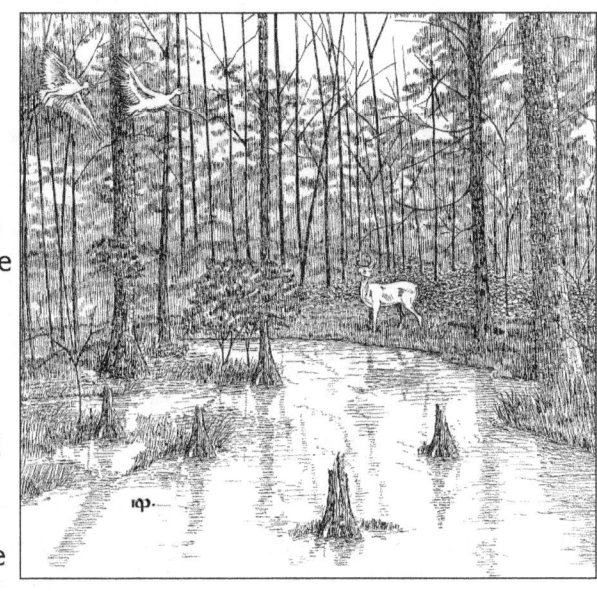

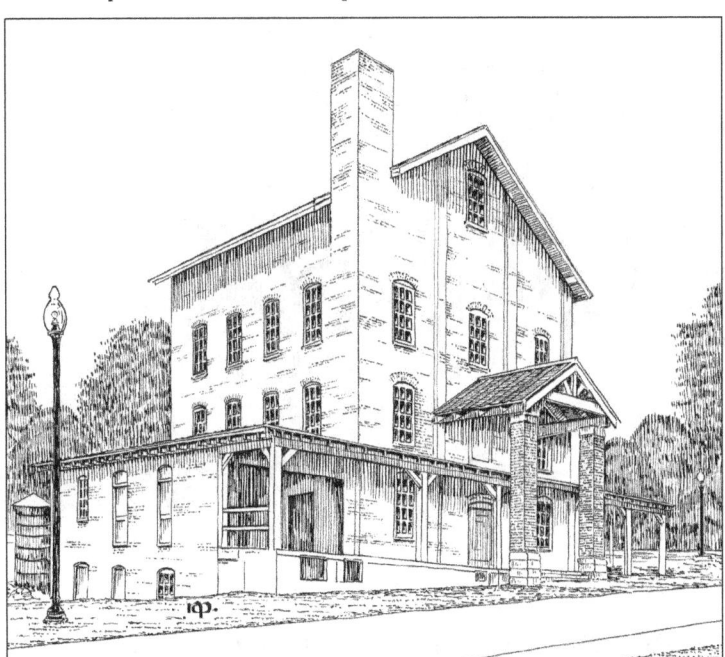

Baughman Mill (Stanford/ Lincoln County) This old mill is a three and one-half story brick structure laid up in American bond. It is located southwest of the L & N Depot in Stanford, close to railroad tracks for convenience of shipping. Sitting above Main Street, the mill was built in 1884 using logs from the first steam mill in the county, known as *Buffalo Mill*. The "old grist mill" was used to make flour, cornmeal and to grind grain to feed cattle. Farmers would bring their grain to be weighed on the side of the building; workers would grind it up and put it in burlap bags for a small fee. The old mill ceased its operation when John Baughman Jr. retired in the 1970s. The landmark building has been completely restored to its original prominent stature and proudly speaks to a time when agriculture played a significant role in the community's colorful heritage.

Black Bears in Kentucky ● Once abundant, the range of the American black bear was significantly reduced by habitat loss in Kentucky by the early 1900s. Bears were essentially eliminated with drastic logging of hardwood forests, unregulated hunting and a lack of protected areas. The return of black bears in Kentucky is a wildlife success story. Black bears are once again abundant and widespread across the state. New forests matured after the extensive logging ceased, and bears from neighboring states recolonized their habitats in Kentucky. Black bears are powerful, large-bodied animals that grow to 4 - 6 feet in length. Typically black with a brown muzzle, adult females weigh up to 170 pounds; males average 250 to 350. The core of the black bear population is concentrated within the mountain areas of Harlan, Letcher, and Pike counties. Bears have become increasingly common in other parts of the state.

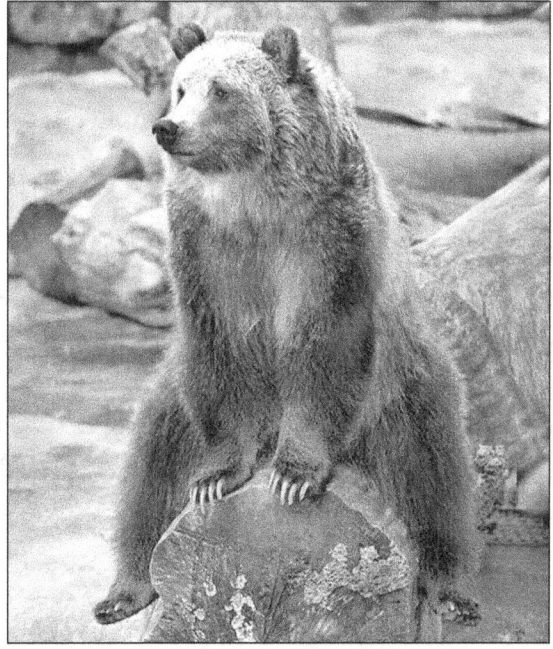

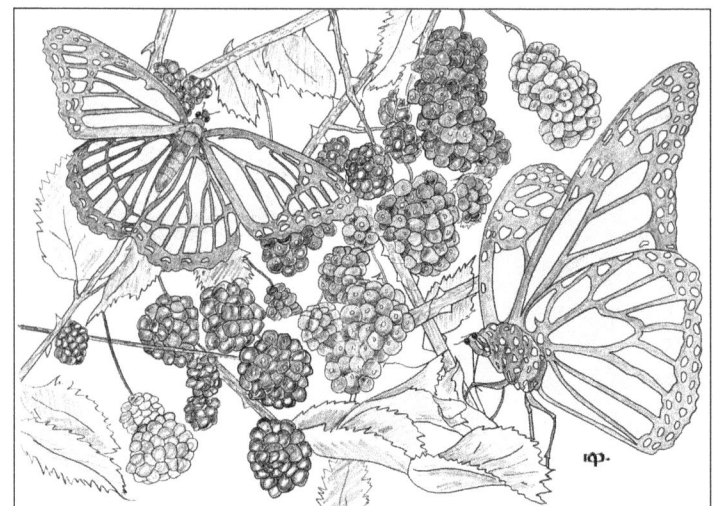

Blackberry was named the official state fruit in 2004. They are delicious raw and are also used in desserts, jams, jellies and wine. Blackberries are a widespread species of berry native throughout the Northern hemisphere. They have numerous (and very sharp) short curved spines on the plant shoots that makes them difficult to harvest.

The Viceroy Butterfly became the official state butterfly of Kentucky in 1990. Viceroy butterflies look like Monarchs; the coloring and pattern are nearly identical. However, a viceroy has a black line across the postmedian hindwing. Viceroys are smaller than the Monarchs, and their flight is faster and more erratic. Viceroys do not migrate. They winter as larvae, and in the spring, they need about 15 days to complete the life cycle and become a butterfly.

Butcher Hollow Home (Van Lear/ Johnson Co.)

Butcher Hollow is a small coal-mining community located between Prestonsburg and Paintsville. Its claim to fame is being the birthplace of country music legend Loretta Lynn, who paid tribute to the area in her song *Coal Miner's Daughter*, in which she sings; "Well, I was born'd a coal miner's daughter...In a cabin on a hill in Butcher Holler." Later in the song, she mentions Van Lear, the larger community in which Butcher Hollow is located. Van Lear was built by the Consolidation Coal Company in the early part of the 20th century, and named for Van Lear Black, a company director. Each year, hundreds of tourists visit the town to see the childhood home of Loretta Lynn, Crystal Gayle, and her siblings. Butcher Hollow is listed as a separate town; however, a hollow in an Eastern Kentucky community is generally referred to the same as a street in a city.

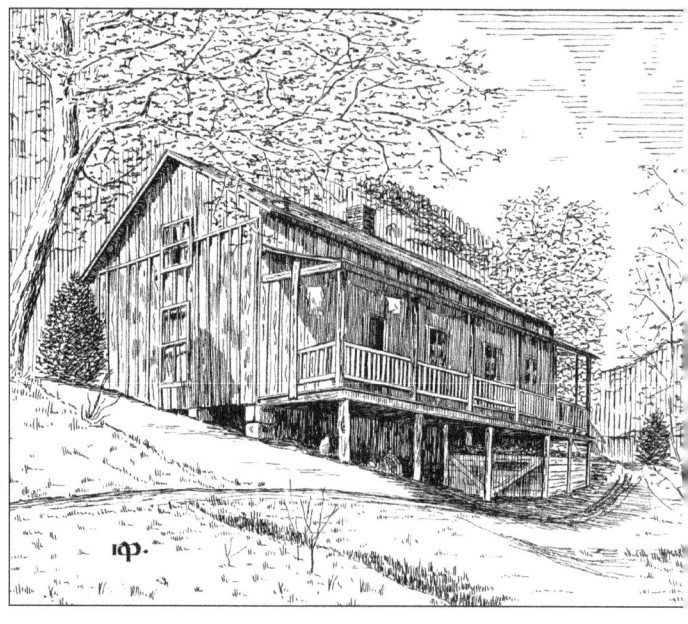

Bybee Pottery (Bybee/ Madison County)

Located in a small rural community on the fringe of the Bluegrass, Bybee Pottery was listed as one of the oldest potteries west of the Appalachian Mountains, with more than 200 years of continuous operation, by six generations of the Cornelison family. Conrad Cornelison, a veteran of the **American Revolution**, settled in the area before 1809 to farm. He made limited quantities of pottery in his spare time, but Conrad's son James Eli is given credit for founding Bybee Pottery as a business in 1845. The farm contains a clay pit of a white, soft, Kaolin-type clay; reported to be one of the highest grades of potting clay in the country. Mixed only with water, it is ground in the old pug mill and stored in a vault where it is kept moist and pliable until thrown on the potter's wheel. Their unique and signature glazes were created on site.

Canon Protecting Cumberland Gap ● The Cumberland Gap was a natural invasion route into the South for Union forces during the Civil War. It also provided access to vulnerable railroads and valuable minerals in Tennessee and Virginia. For the South, it was a gateway for an invasion of Kentucky. Military possession of Cumberland Gap changed hands four times during the Civil War. The Confederates first fortified the Gap in August 1861. Union forces, under General Morgan, took the Gap in June 1862. Under General Stevenson, the Confederates evacuated the Union troops from the Gap in September 1862 as they moved through the area and pushed on into the Bluegrass. The final exchange came when General Burnside accepted the surrender of Confederate General Frazer there in September 1863.

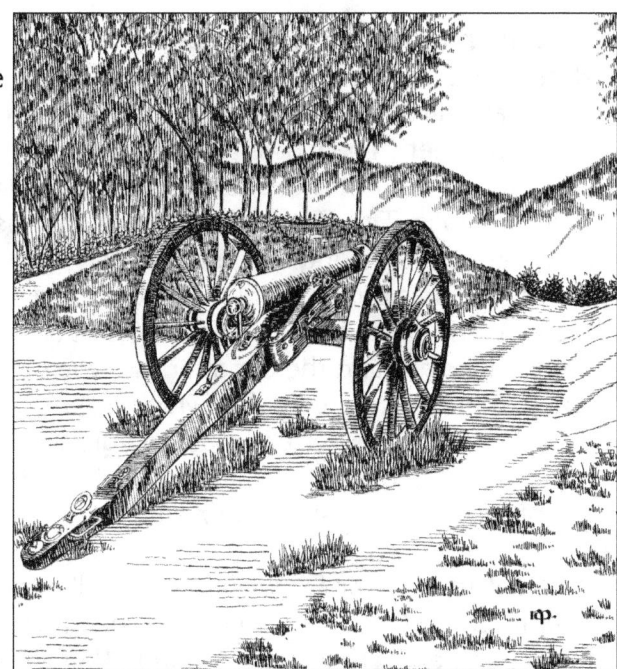

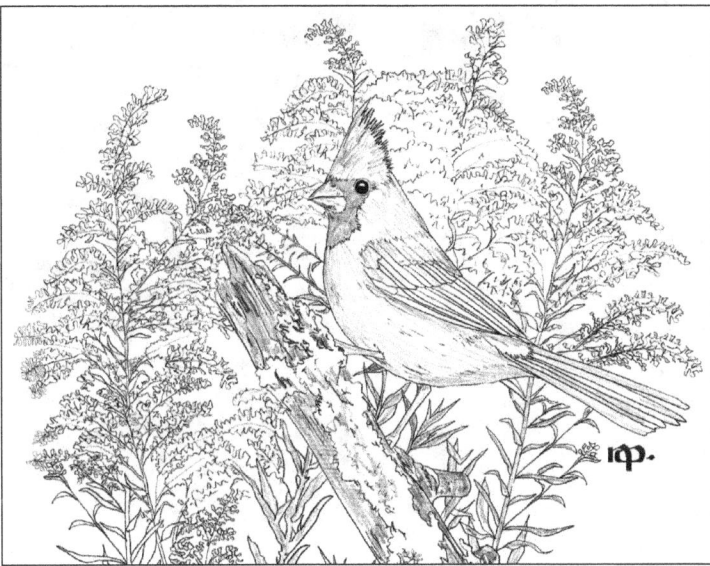

The **Northern Cardinal** was named official state bird of Kentucky in 1926. It is one of America's favorite songbirds. Cardinals are distinctive in appearance; male cardinals are a brilliant scarlet red, females a buffy brown - both have a jet-black mask, heavy bill, and a pronounced crest. The male defends his 4-acre territory aggressively. Northern cardinals breed 2-3 times each season. The female builds the nest and tends the hatchlings while the male brings food. The male then takes care of this brood while the female moves on to a new nest to lay a second clutch of eggs. The cardinal is designated as the state bird for seven states.

Goldenrod was designated official state flower of Kentucky in 1926.

Columbus-Belmont Battlefield State Park (Hickman County)

Located on the banks of the Mississippi River, at the old site of Columbus in Hickman County, this historic area became a part of the Kentucky State Parks System in 1934. The *Union* plan for conquest of the South in the *Civil War*, involved the Mississippi River. To prevent that strategy, Gen. Leonidas Polk, C.S.A., seized and heavily fortified the high bluff above Columbus. A great chain more than a mile long was stretched across the river to prevent passage by Union gunboats. The giant chain was attached to a 6-ton anchor from a sea-going vessel on the Kentucky shore, and 140 guns were placed to sweep the river. The Missouri bank of the river at Belmont was also occupied by a force of the Confederate army.

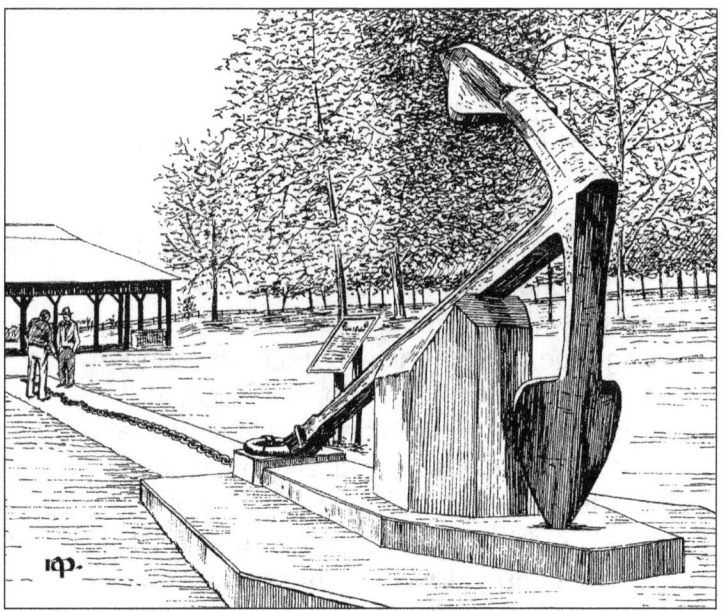

Corvette was designated as the official state sports car for Kentucky in 2010. The National Corvette Museum is located in Bowling Green. The Corvette for this drawing is parked in front of the famous rock fences of the Bluegrass. The Chevrolet Corvette car has been produced through 7 generations. The first model was a convertible, introduced at the GM Motorama in 1953. Myron Scott is credited for naming the car after the type of small, maneuverable warship which is called a corvette. The Corvette is manufactured in Kentucky and is listed as the official sports car of the Commonwealth of Kentucky.

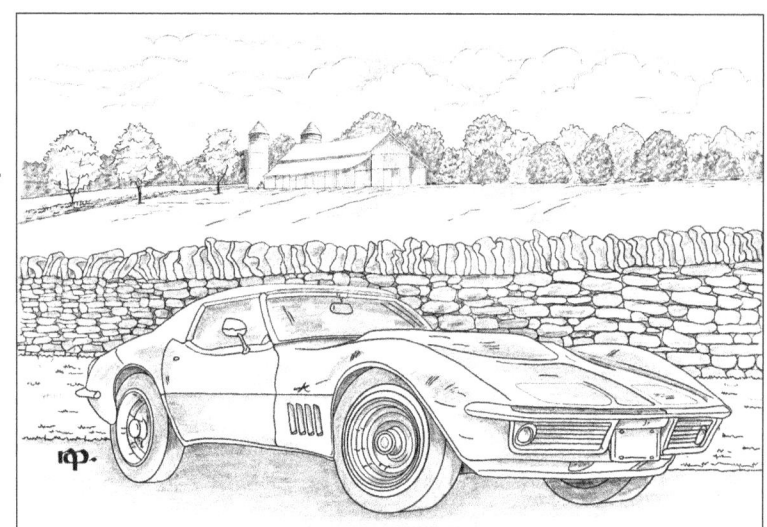

Kentucky Deer Population was well over 800,000 deer in 2018. Deer were an important stable for the first humans to enter Kentucky, around 10,000 years ago. The deer herd was hunted to near extinction in the early 1900s, with only a very few left in the western part of the state. Diligent conservation efforts restored the deer to several thousand by the early 1940s. By the late 1960s the herd was estimated at about 35,000 and growing very slowly. With good management the herd grew to 610,000 by 1999. Over a period of 52 years, more than 10,000 of the white-tailed deer were relocated throughout the state, most coming from Caldwell, Christian, Lyon, and Trigg Counties. At the turn of the century, the deer population had stabilized and deer hunting was allowed across the entire state. Elk are also native to Kentucky, but were gone from the state and most other eastern states since the mid-1800s. With the success of the deer program, Kentucky began to restock elk into eastern Kentucky in 1997 and by 2018 boasted the largest herd of elk in the entire eastern United States with a herd of 12,000 elk.

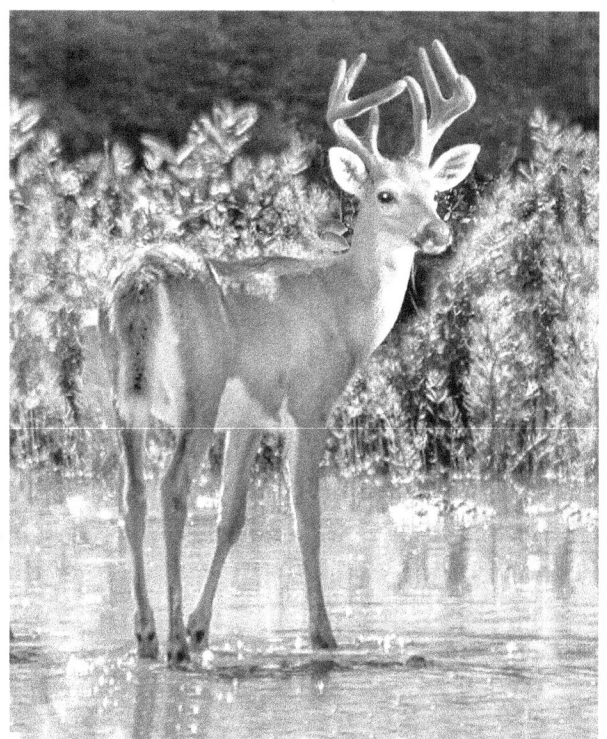

Gray Squirrel was designated the official state wild animal of Kentucky in 1968. The gray squirrel is a native mammal of the rodent family that has been in North America for over 37 million years. The eastern gray squirrel is most frequently seen east of the Mississippi River. In autumn, the gray squirrel spends each day gathering nuts and seeds and hiding them so it will have enough food to last through the winter. The squirrel buries food in hundreds of different locations. The squirrel cleans each nut or seed before it is hidden and leaves a scent that the squirrel can find later in the winter, even under heavy snow. Squirrels are responsible for planting more trees than humans. **Tulip Poplar** was designated official state tree of Kentucky in 1994.

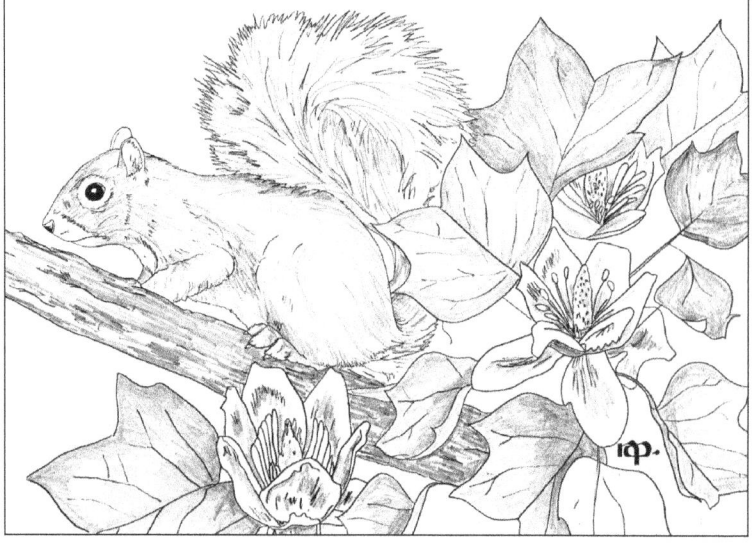

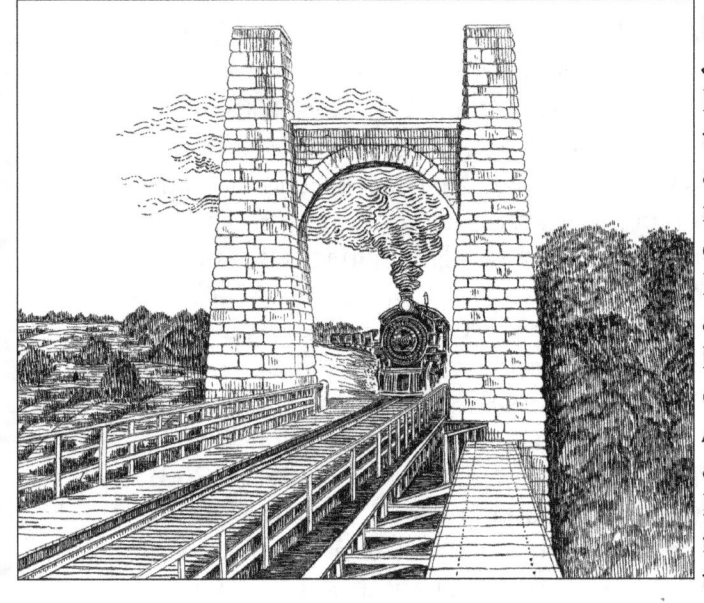

High Bridge was designed as a suspension bridge by John Roebling, who created the famous Brooklyn Bridge in New York City. Huge stone towers were built to hold cables in 1851, but work on the bridge was abandoned during the Civil War. Construction was resumed by the Cincinnati Southern Railway, and it opened in 1877. The bridge was dedicated in 1879 by President Rutherford B. Hayes. The 275/308-foot tall and 1,125-foot bridge crosses the deep gorge of the Kentucky River between Jessamine and Mercer counties. It is the first cantilever bridge built on the American continent and became an immediate tourist attraction as the highest railroad bridge in the world. In 1911 the bridge was rebuilt using the same foundations and without stopping rail service. In 1929 the large twin towers were removed.

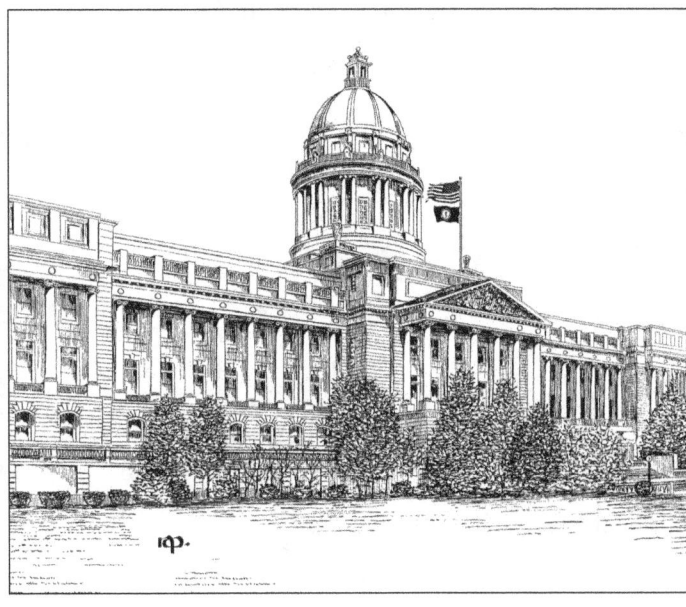

Kentucky Capitol (Frankfort/ Franklin County) was dedicated June 1, 1910. Frankfort was the first permanent capital created west of the Alleghenies after Kentucky was admitted as the 15th State of the Union in 1792. It is the 4th permanent structure built to house the offices of state government. The first three Capitols were built on the site in the center of town where the *Old Statehouse* stands. The first two structures were destroyed by fire. In 1905, the *General Assembly* selected a 34-acre site for a new capitol across the river from the old one, away from the crowded downtown. The cornerstone was laid June 16, 1906, and the Capitol was completed in 1910 at a total cost (land, construction, and furnishings) of $1,820,000. It was built entirely by hand and it is considered one of the biggest bargains in public buildings in the Untied States.

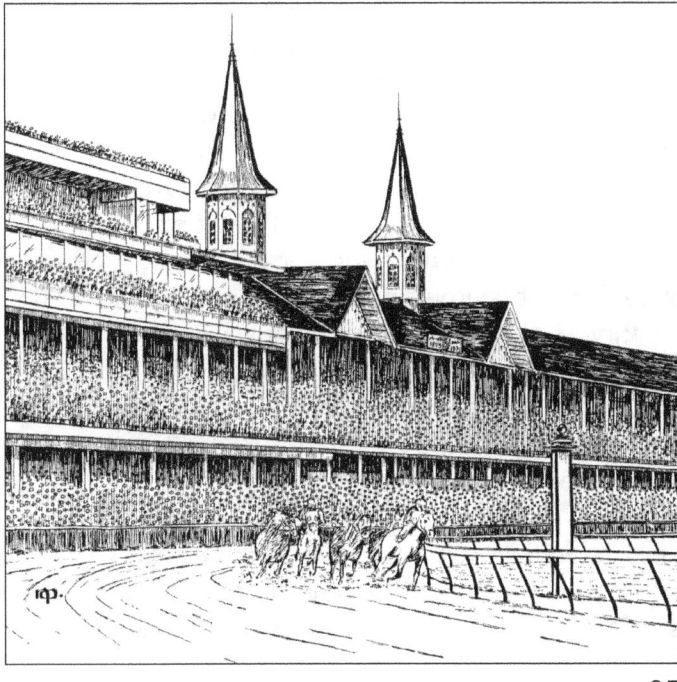

Kentucky Derby is run the first Saturday of May each year at Churchill Downs. The Derby has run every year since 1875 when the 180-acre racetrack was first opened by Colonel M. Lewis Clark, who was inspired by the race tracks in England. With some friends, he formed the Kentucky Jockey Club and built the course. In 1875, ten thousand people watched as **Aristides** won the first Kentucky Derby. The Derby soon became America's supreme racing event and the first leg of the ultra-prestigious Triple Crown of racing. Some 200,000 spectators crowd into the park for the Derby each year and millions around the world view the activities on television. Since 1904 the Derby winner has been honored with a blanket of American Beauty roses. It was dubbed *Run for the Roses* in 1925 by Bill Corum, a New York sports writer.

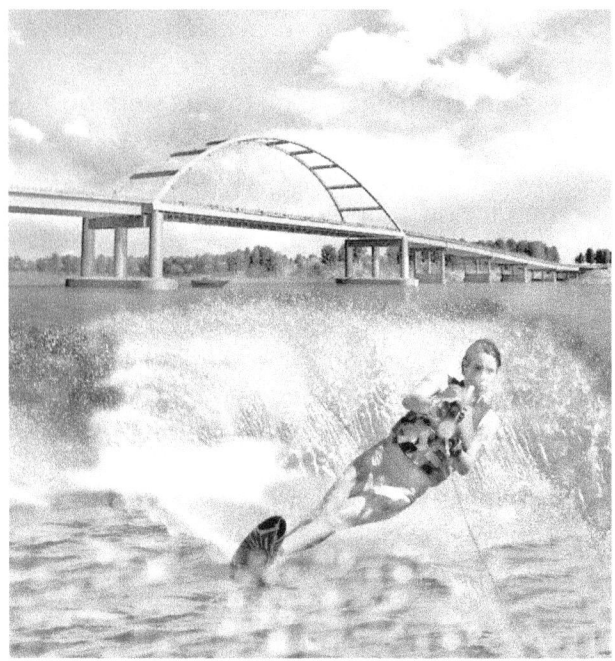

Kentucky Lake is a magnet for vacationers and fishermen, with recreation use amounting to over 17 million visits each year. Along its nearly 2400 miles of cove-studded shoreline are many boat docks and resorts, 4 state parks, the Tennessee National Wildlife Refuge, 48 public access areas, 2 county parks, 5 municipal parks, 2 state wildlife management areas, 10 group camps, 92 commercial recreation areas, and 3 small wildlife areas. Construction of Kentucky Dam began in 1938 and was completed six years later, in 1944. At the peak of construction, TVA had nearly 5,000 men at work building the dam. The dam, which is more than a mile long and rises 206 feet above its foundation, required 1,356,000 cubic yards of concrete and 5,582,000 cubic yards of earth and rock fill. The project cost about $118 million. It helps provide flood protection to 6 million acres of land in the lower Ohio and Mississippi valleys.

Kentucky Spotted Bass was designated as the official state fish of Kentucky in 1956. The spotted bass is also called spotty. It is a species of freshwater fish of the sunfish family and is native to the Mississippi River basin and across the Gulf states, from Texas through Florida. It is often mistaken for the similar and more common largemouth bass. The most convenient way to distinguish between largemouth bass and a spotted bass is by the size of the mouth. A spotted bass resembles a largemouth bass in coloration but will have a smaller mouth. The Kentucky Spotted Bass can reach an overall length of 25 inches, with weights of up to 11 pounds, and can reach an age of seven years. It is noted for the rows of dark spots below the lateral line, which give it the name.

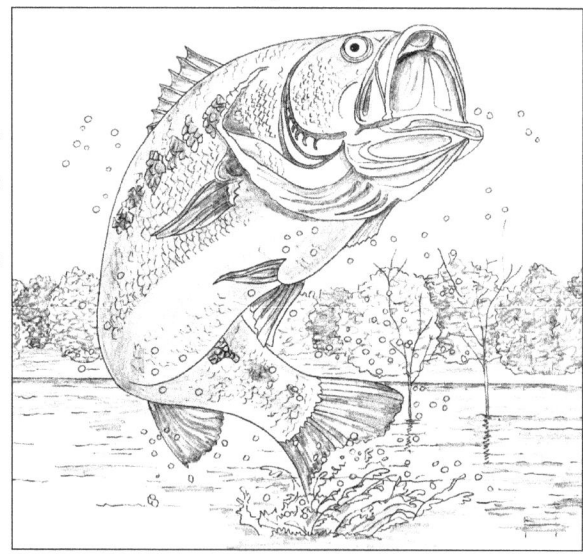

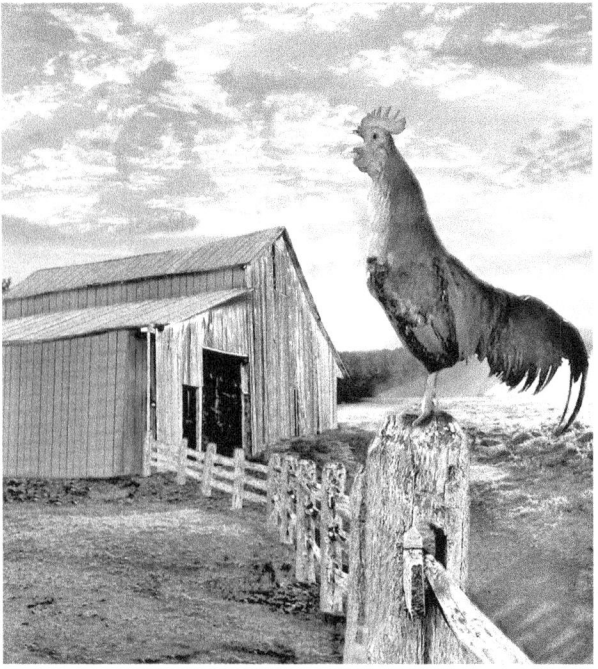

Kentucky Sunrise is an iconic symbol of the rural Kentucky farm. The frontier wilderness opened as a gateway to the west in the late 1700s when colonists along the east coast of the New World became restless and curious about the vast expanse of land beyond the mountains. Because of the rugged travel conditions, it was necessary to be self-sufficient once one passed through the Cumberland Gap. Many of those early explorers became settlers in Kentucky. For the next century, the image of the pioneer was a rural family on a small farm. It was not until the mid-1900s that industry busted into the commonwealth. Fruit of the Loom established a home here in the 1940s, to manufacture underwear. General Electric, Corning Glass, Ford Motor Company, IBM, Square D, and Rand McNally soon followed. Kentucky became a prime location for industry, yet the small family farms continue to dot the state and the infamous crowing rooster is still as much a part of everyday life as well as a part of our colorful heritage.

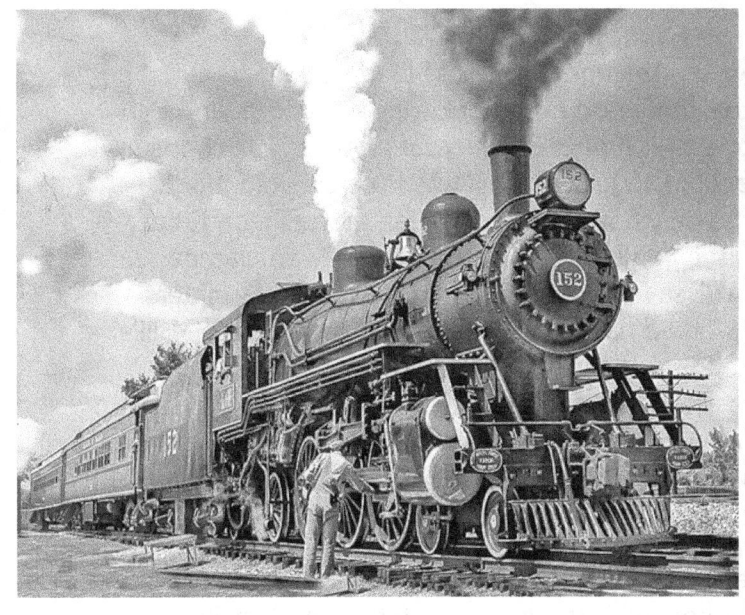

L&N 152 - Official State Steam Locomotive was restored by the volunteer members of the **Kentucky Railway Museum.** This non-profit organization has a mission to educate the public regarding the history and heritage of Kentucky's railroads and the people who built them. L&N 152 was retired on February 17, 1953, and donated by the L&N to the newly formed Kentucky Railway Museum for preservation in 1957. Originally located in Louisville, the Museum moved to New Haven in 1990, with the purchase of 17 miles of the former L&N Lebanon Branch line. L&N #152 is one of the five Pacific (4-6-2) type locomotives built for L & N Railroad in 1905. Today it is one of only three steam locomotives remaining from "The Old Reliable" L&N railroad and is the only surviving L&N passenger steam locomotive.

L & N Depot where passengers and freight boarded the train for other parts of the country in a time when a train was THE best method for travel; from right after the Civil War, a little more than 100 years, until the late 1980s. The depot represents a more active period of railroading and commercial ventures. The structure was generally of frame construction and basically rectangular in shape. It was most often situated on a brick foundation. The front side faced the tracks, while the rear extended toward a parking lot. This one-story depot is characteristic of the more highly stylized L & N railroad depots constructed all along the train lines - especially throughout Kentucky.

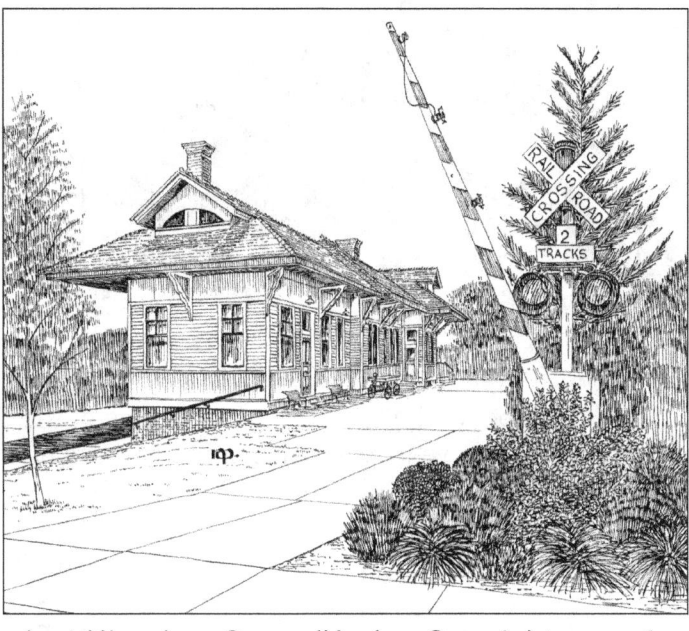

Log Rock at Kingdom Come (Harlan County) is one of the major natural features found at Kingdom Come State Park near Cumberland. The park proudly claims some of the most extraordinary rock formations in the state. This long narrow natural sandstone arch looks like an immense log spanning a gorge. This giant rock soars 290 feet into the air at a 45-degree angle. The park crowns the crest of Pine Mountain at an elevation of 2,700 feet, and it preserves more than 1,200 acres of unspoiled wilderness. Originally known as **Raven Rock Park**, it was renamed in 1961 after the popular novel, *The Little Shepherd of Kingdom Come* by Kentucky author John Fox Jr. Pine Mountain is taller than the hills to its north, so the view from several overlooks reveals an endless ocean of foliage representing the extreme variety of growth in this pristine mountain wilderness. The Civilian Conservation Corps constructed 17 miles of trails between 1933 and 1937, and the Kentucky Division of Forestry added 21 miles of new trail during 1962.

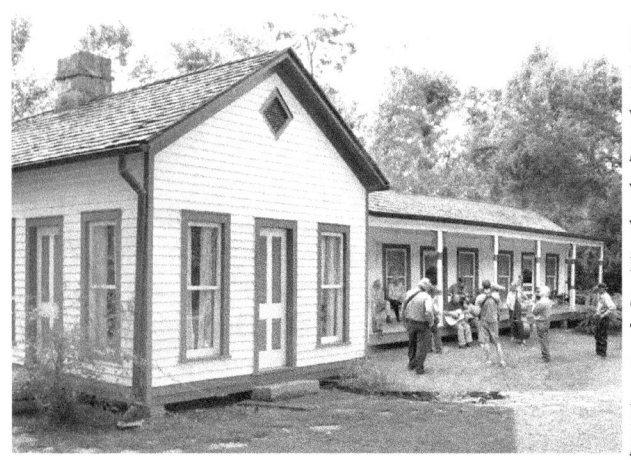

Monroe Homeplace (Ohio County)

Known as "the homeplace of bluegrass music," this was the childhood home of country music legend Bill Monroe, the "Father of Bluegrass Music." This house was built in 1917 when Bill was five years old, but it was the only home he knew. High atop Pigeon Ridge, it was the centerpiece of an 800-acre farm. James and Malissa Monroe had six sons and two daughters. They worked hard to make their farm successful. Bill's "Uncle Pen," and two of his brothers were also professional musicians, Birch and Charlie Monroe. Bill Monroe was a star of the **Grand Ole Opry** for over 50 years. He remains the only person to be inducted into three Halls of Fame: Bluegrass, Country, and Rock and Roll. He was presented with the *National Medal of Arts* by President Bill Clinton in 1995.

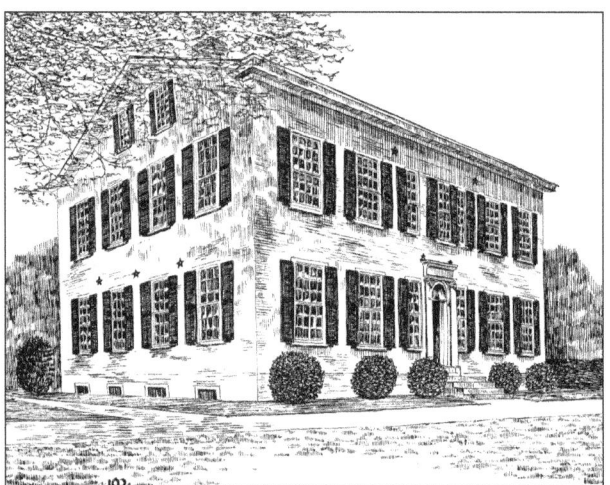

Federal Hill (Bardstown/ Nelson County), the manor house for the great plantation of John Rowan, was the inspiration for the ballad by Stephen Foster and the nucleus for the state park. *My Old Kentucky Home* was adopted as the official state song in 1928. This splendid mansion was completed in 1818 and Rowan's cousin, Stephen Foster, made it the symbol for Kentucky when he wrote "My Old Kentucky Home" during a visit in 1852. The song captured the hearts of the entire nation as exemplifying the traditional character of the South. It became the state song for Kentucky in 1928, some 64 years after Foster died at the young age of 37. Rowan served as Secretary of State, member of the U. S. Congress, judge of the Court of Appeals and U. S. Senator. He died in 1843, nearly ten years before his home became an international landmark.

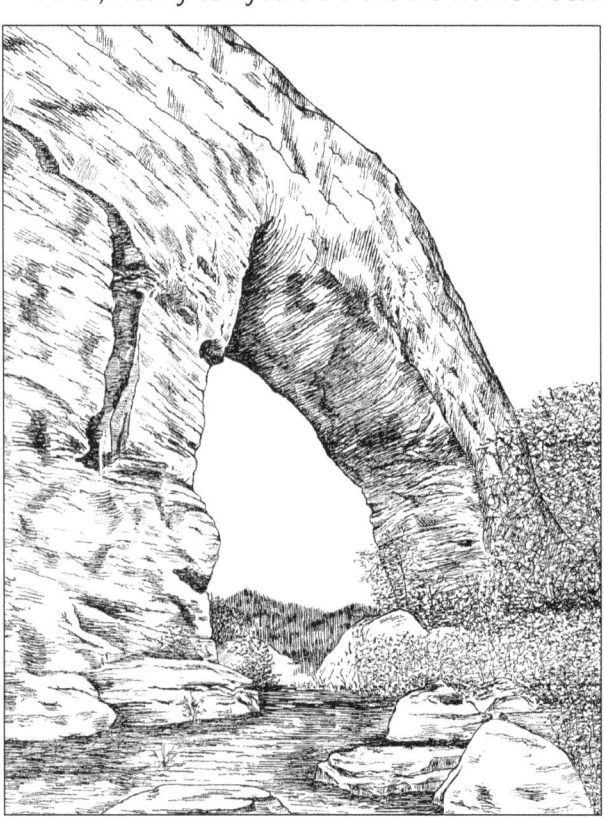

Natural Bridge (Slade/ Powell County) has exhilarated Americans long before the pioneers first discovered this wilderness. The entire area is covered with artifacts from civilizations that precede the modern Indians. According to the calculations made by several geologists, it actually took more than one million years for disintegrating action of wind, mist, rain, and frost to form a stunning arch over 78 feet in length and 65 feet high. It includes more than fifteen million pounds of suspended rock. The stone in the center is over 20 feet wide, and it is flat enough to serve as a bridge. The area was developed by the Louisville & Nashville Railroad around the turn of the century as a terminus for weekend train excursions from the city. The entire area was turned over to the state by L & N about 1926 to be cultivated as one of the four original state parks. The park has 2,400 acres in the Daniel Boone National Forest. The ridge, of which this reddish rock of the Paleozoic era is a part, forms the borderline which separates the Kentucky counties of Powell and Wolfe.

Newport Aquarium (on the Levee in Newport)

Although it is far from the ocean, Newport Aquarium provides visitors an opportunity to view the underwater world of the sea. Shark lovers are fascinated by a shark tunnel where sharks swim overhead, Shark Central where visitors pet small sharks and the Shark Bridge which traverses the top of the shark tank. Newport Aquarium is also home to four rare Shark Rays. Other exhibits show the diversity of aquatic habitats, including a coral reef, river environments, and a fascinating jellyfish exhibit. The Tide Pool allows visitors to touch creatures like sea stars and crabs. Newport Aquarium is also home to several other species: the largest alligator in the US outside of Florida, 17 species of penguins, exotic frogs, and adorable otters. Visitors can touch turtles in the Turtle Corral. The aquarium has 70 exhibits and 14 galleries, including five seamless acrylic tunnels totaling over 200 feet in length. The aquarium showcases thousands of animals from around the world in 1,000,000 gallons of water.

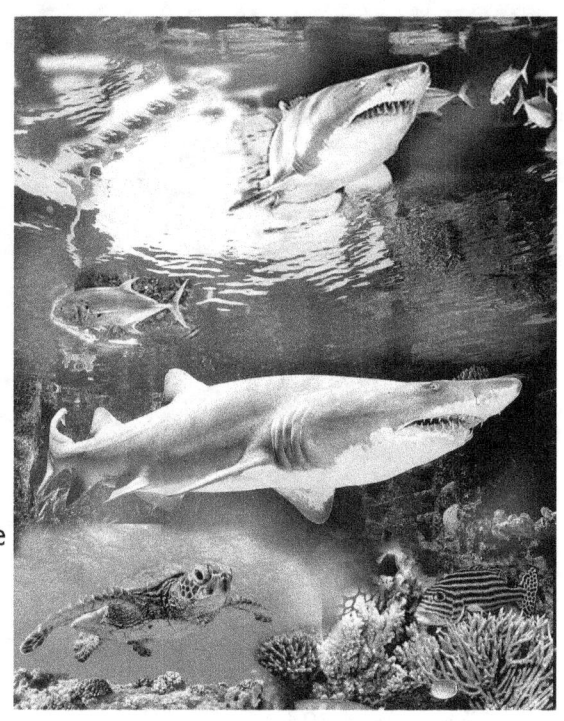

Old Mulkey Meetinghouse (Tompkinsville/ Monroe Co.)

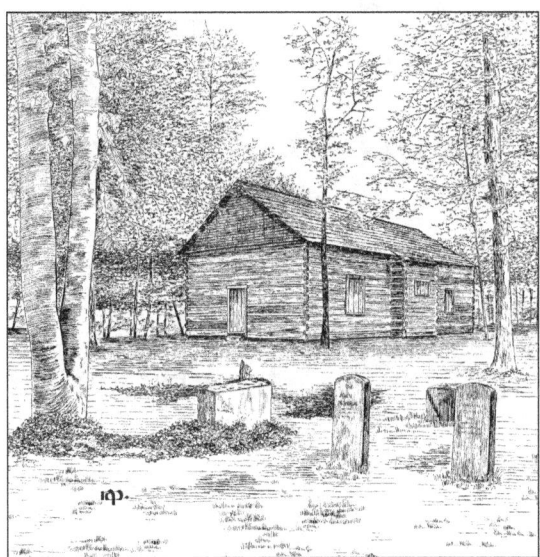

In 1773 Philip Mulkey and a group of Baptists from North and South Carolina settled about two miles from the town of Tompkinsville. This historic old house of worship was constructed in 1798 of half-hewn logs, chinked with rocks and mud. The Mulkey Meetinghouse has twelve corners, representing the twelve Apostles and symbolic of the twelve Tribes of Israel. No heating arrangements were made. The burial ground next to the church includes the grave of Hannah Boone, sister of Daniel Boone, plus the graves of many pioneer families and soldiers of the Revolutionary War. The area was settled before Kentucky became a state in 1792, but Monroe County was created in 1820, and named in honor of President Monroe. The county seat is named for Daniel Tompkins, Vice-president under Pres. James Monroe; the only such situation known in the U. S.

Pennyrile State Forest (Dawson Springs/ Hopkins Co.)

has some of the most beautiful forested lands in the commonwealth. The 15,331-acre Pennyrile Forest became a part of the Kentucky State Parks System in 1954. In the 1930s the National Parks Service and the Works Progress Administration (WPA) developed a 300-acre tract for recreational purposes. The WPA continued its work in the area until 1937 when the Kentucky Division of State Parks took responsibility for the land on an annual agreement basis. Pennyrile now has 863 acres with a 56-acre lake. The state had a new lodge constructed and with the completion of Lake Beshear in 1962, gave the area a 712-acre lake located in both Caldwell and Christian Counties. The 24-room rustic wood and stone lodge at *Pennyrile Forest State Resort Park* sits serenely on a high cliff overlooking Pennyrile Lake near Dawson Springs.

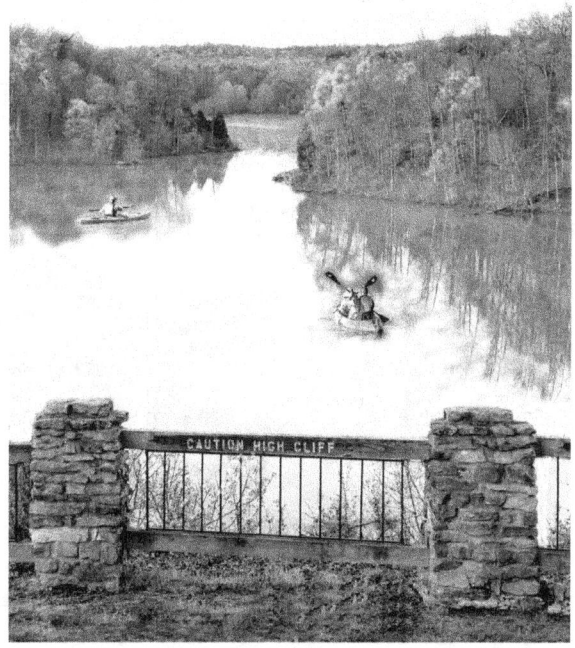

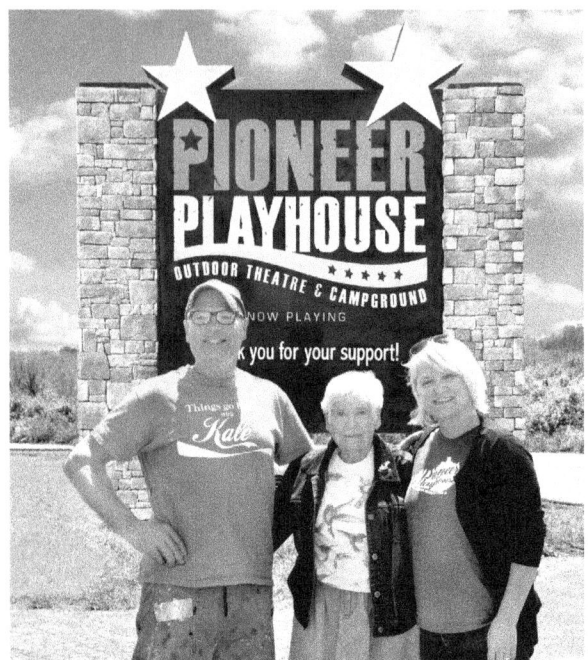

Pioneer Playhouse (Danville/ Boyle County)
Eben C. Henson brought *Broadway* to the *Bluegrass* in 1950, when he founded Pioneer Playhouse. It is the oldest outdoor theatre in Kentucky. Colonel Henson was instrumental in pioneering outdoor theatre across the state. During the 50s and 60s, Pioneer Playhouse also received national attention as the "King of Summer Stocks" in all the New York trade magazines. In 1962 it became the first theatre in the nation to be accorded the legal status of State Theatre by an act of legislation. It continues to be a popular theatre venue and training ground for aspiring actors, offering live performances June through August. The theatre is still run by members of the Henson family; Robby is the Artistic Director, Charlotte (co-founder) is the producer, and Heather is the Managing Director.

Raven Run Nature Preserve (Lexington/ Fayette County)
This unique 734-acre nature sanctuary is dedicated to the preservation of the Kentucky River Palisades, early history of the region, and the protection of the animals and over 600 species of plants found within its boundaries. More than 10 miles of hiking trails provide access to streams, meadows, woodlands and creek ecosystems as well as historic and geologic features. Part of the property was acquired with funds from the Kentucky Heritage Land Conservation Fund. Numerous 19th-century remnants of early settlers, as well as indigenous plants and animals, allow visitors to become acquainted with and appreciate the natural world. The sanctuary also accommodates more than 200 species of birds. Activities are limited to the trail system in order to protect the flora and fauna of the sanctuary. The Raven Run Nature Center is located at the beginning of the trail system featuring displays and a variety of "hands-on" exhibits. Pamphlets about history, birds, mammals, ferns, and aspects of the sanctuary are available.

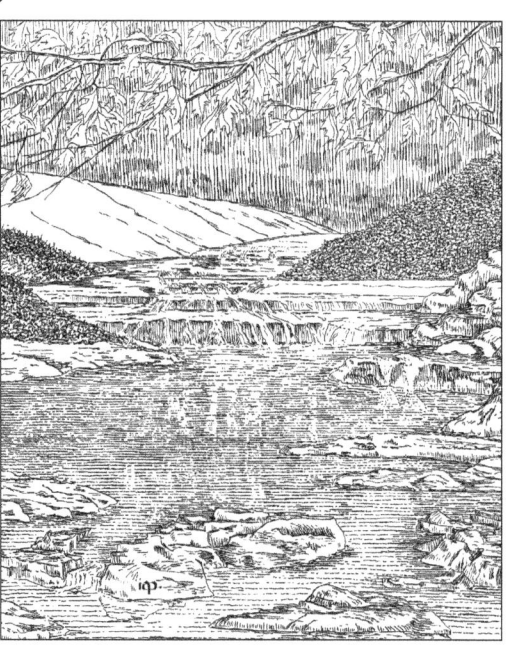

Red River Museum (Clay City/ Powell County) Clay City National Bank was established in 1890. The building was erected a year earlier to house banking operations which had been created by the logging industry boom. Clay City became the heart of a vast industrial complex during the 1890s. From 1908 until 1938 the Clay City Post Office was housed in the back section of the bank building. The Bank ceased operations in 1944, and the building had a great variety of various occupants over the next few decades. The old Clay City National Bank Building was listed on the *National Register of Historic Places* in 1978. It was restored as headquarters and the museum for the Red River Historical Society, which preserves the cultural heritage of Powell County and the Red River area with exhibits ranging from prehistoric artifacts to 19th-century relics.

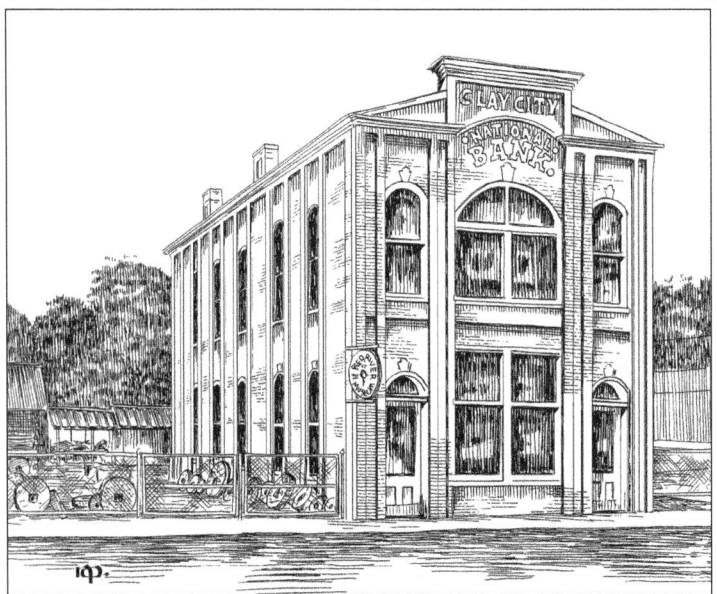

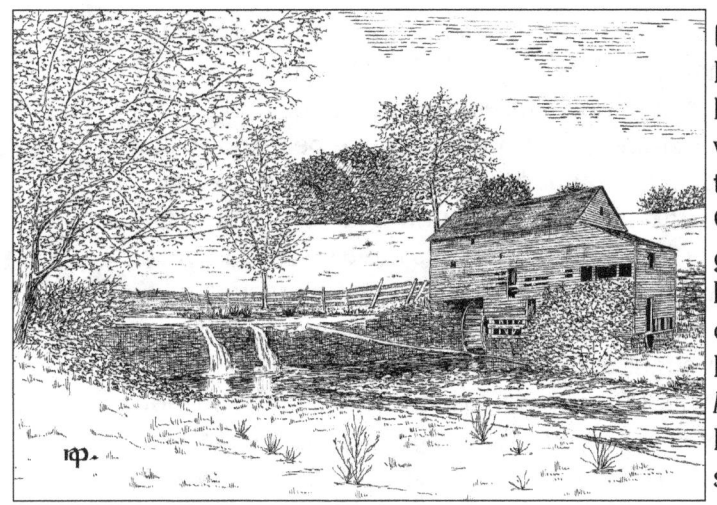

Ryman's Mill (Lexington/ Fayette County)

Ryman's Mill near South Elkhorn Creek on the Lexington, Harrodsburg and Perryville Turnpike, was built by Jacob Ryman and operated well into the late 1800s by his son Robert. South Elkhorn Creek's continuous flow and accessibility made it a good location for water-powered grist mills in the late 18th and early 19th centuries. Four were completed in the area by 1795 including John Higbee's Mill, Abraham Bowman's Mill, Ryman's Mill, and Captain James Parker's Mill. The buhrs of Ryman's Mill were imported from Europe, and it is said that Ryman removed one from the mill after seventy years of constant use. The black locust frame supporting the buhrs was still intact. This old grinding device was made almost entirely of wood; even the large ponderous gears and wheel that step up the power of the running water.

Swinging Bridge (Loyall/ Harlan County)

was one of the last such landmarks remaining in an area where hundreds of such bridges were necessary just a few years ago. Numerous creeks flow out of the mountains to join with the Clover Fork and Cumberland rivers, which join forces near the city of Harlan. This bridge gave way to the flood control project which has been in progress since the early 1990s. Because of the unusual terrain in most parts of the region, homes were built on one side of a creek, and either the creek itself was originally used as a road, or the roadbed had to be built on the opposite side of the waterway. This condition created hundreds of small bridges, most often a swinging bridge, used

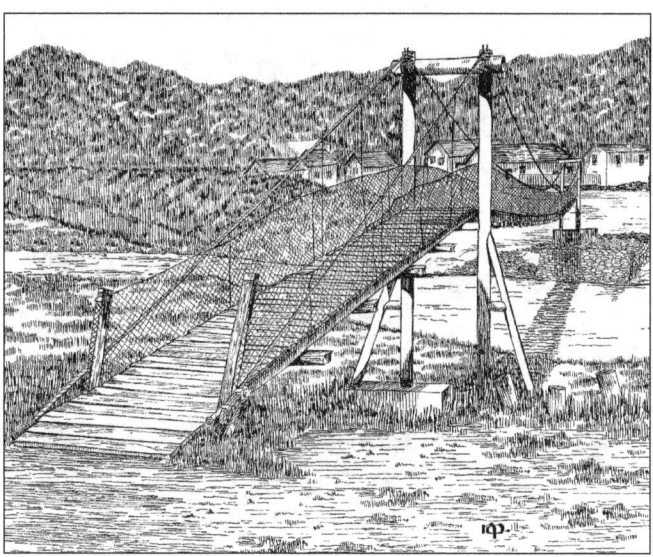

by one or two families or a small community of families. This old bridge at Loyall is a typical symbol of that heritage that was a very necessary part of the development of our country.

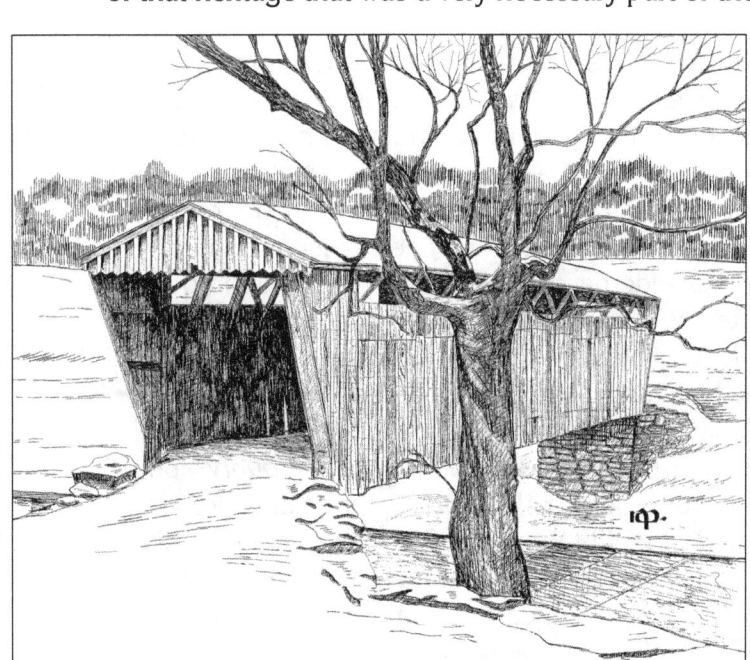

Switzer Covered Bridge (Franklin County)

This historic bridge over North Elkhorn Creek in Franklin County, was designated the official state covered bridge of Kentucky in 1998. The bridge is 60 feet long, and eleven feet wide; resting on sturdy stone supports. The side walls stop about two feet from the edge of the roof. The contractor was George Hockensmith. Built about 1855 and restored in 1906, then closed to traffic in 1954. The bridge was again restored in 1997 after a flood swept the bridge off its foundation. In Kentucky, you'll find a dozen covered bridges open to the public and one on private property, each is listed on the *National Register of Historic Places*. Once numbering as many as 700 across the state, these "timbered tunnels" were eventually destroyed, or simply replaced with modern structures.

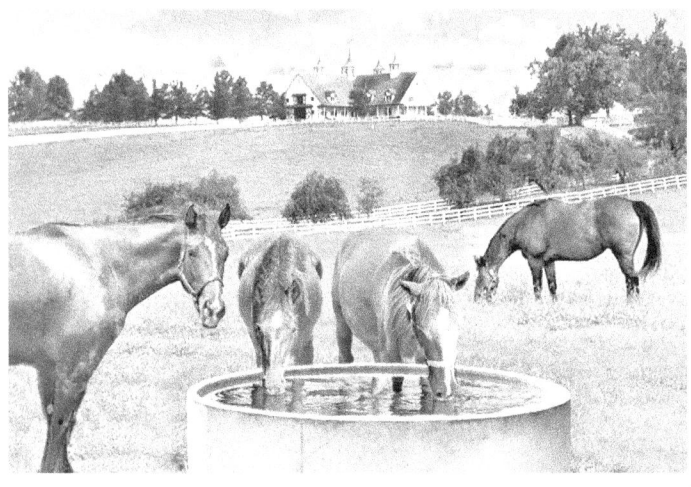

The Thoroughbred became the official state horse of Kentucky in 1996. Thoroughbred is a breed of horse celebrated for speed and endurance. Thoroughbreds are best known as racehorses but are popular in other equestrian sports such as polo, hunting, and eventing. Off the track, thoroughbreds are also used in police work as well as equine-assisted therapy. All thoroughbreds trace their lineage to 3 stallions brought to Great Britain from the Middle East over 300 years ago. Known as the "Foundation Stallions" they are the *Byerly Turk,* the *Darley Arabian,* and the *Godolphin Arabian*. They were bred to native horses to produce a breed that could sustain speed over an extended distance. All American thoroughbred pedigrees are documented in the *American Stud Book*, first compiled by Colonel Sanders Bruce of Kentucky in 1873.

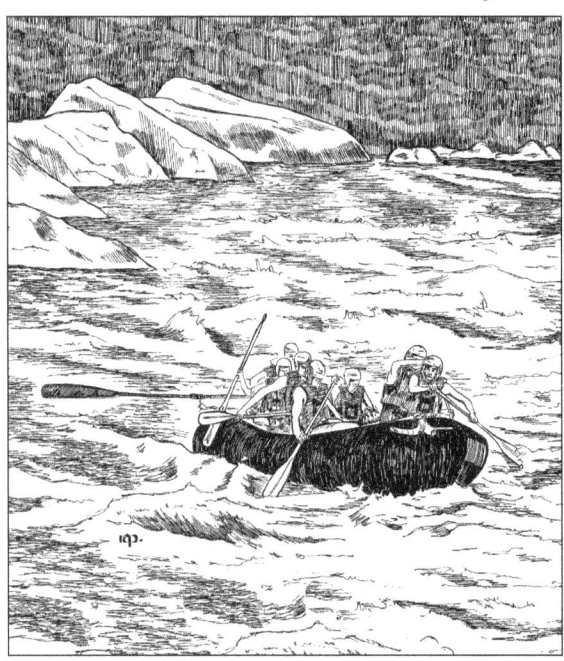

White Water Rafting in a state known for horses, whiskey, and unique southern accents. There are three outstanding rivers for whitewater rafting in Kentucky. They are located within a few hours from major urban areas such as Knoxville and Lexington. Most trips are one-day in length, but they range in difficulty from mild float trips on Elkhorn Creek to some of the most challenging whitewater in the United States on the Russell Fork of the Big Sandy River. During the summer months, rafting is a cooler alternative to hiking and bike riding. Cumberland River rafting trips float through the rapids on a run from the *Cumberland Falls State Resort Park*. Elkhorn Creek Rafting is great for beginners; easy to access, have fun rapids, and are suitable for the entire family. Big Sandy River Rafting on the Russell Fork is one of the most daredevil run stretches of whitewater in the U.S., with multiple drops and rapids that look like waterfalls.

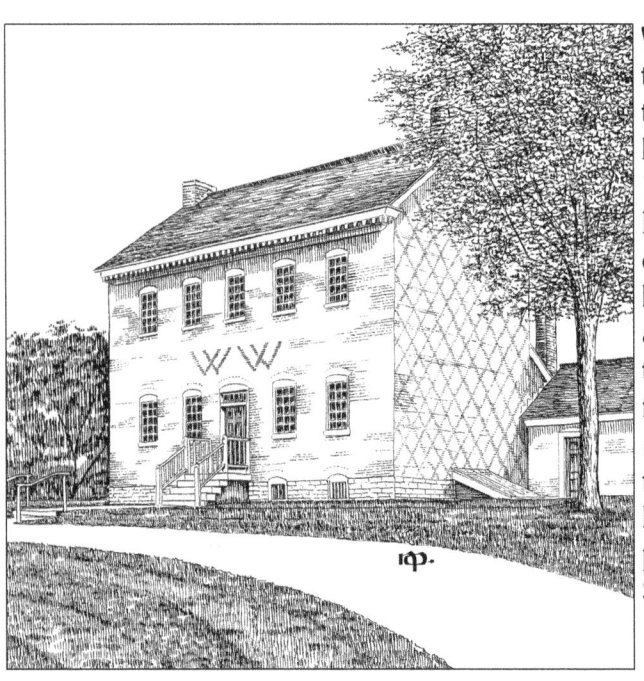

Whitley House (Crab Orchard/ Lincoln Co.) is the oldest brick house in Kentucky. It was built in the 1780s by Col. William Whitley, who came to Kentucky from the more civilized part of Virginia in 1775. Often used as a haven of safety from roving Indians, they dubbed their fine residence "Guardian of the Wilderness Road." Over the front door, the letters WW for William Whitley are visible in brick of a lighter color. EW for his wife Esther Whitley is over the back door. The house passed out of the Whitley family after Colonel Whitley was killed at the *Battle of the Thames* in 1813. Both *Whitley County*, and the county seat of *Williamsburg* are named in his honor. In 1788 Whitley laid out a racetrack on his property. This was the first racetrack in Kentucky. Situated just southeast of Stanford, the *William Whitley House* is open as a State Shrine.